**TEACHER'S PET PUBLICATIONS**

PUZZLE PACK
for
Native Son

based on the book by
Richard Wright

Written by
William T. Collins

© 2005 Teacher's Pet Publications
All Rights Reserved

The materials in this packet are copyrighted
by Teacher's Pet Publications, Inc.

These pages may be duplicated by the purchaser
for use in the purchaser's own classroom.

Copying any of these materials and distributing them
for any other purpose is a violation of the copyright laws.

© 2005 Teacher's Pet Publications, Inc.
www.tpet.com

INTRODUCTION
If you already own the LitPlan for this title, this Puzzle Pack will refresh your Unit Resource Materials and Vocabulary Resource Materials sections plus give you additional materials you can substitute into the tests. If you do not already have a complete LitPlan, these pages will give you some supplemental materials to use with your own plan. There are two main groups of materials: one set for unit words (such as characters' names, symbols, places, etc.) and one set for vocabulary words associated with the book.

WORD LIST
There is a word list for both the unit words and the vocabulary words. These lists show you which words are being used in the materials and the clues or definitions being used for those words. You may want to give students a word list with clues/definitions to help them, or you may want students to only have a word list (without clues/definitions) if you want them to work a little harder. Both are available for duplication. The word lists can also be your "calling key" for the bingo games.

FILL IN THE BLANK AND MATCHING
There are 4 each of the fill in the blank and matching worksheets for both the unit and vocabulary words. These pages can be used either as extra worksheets for students or as objective parts of a unit test. They can be done individually if students need extra help or as a whole class activity to review the material covered.

MAGIC SQUARES
The magic squares not only reinforce the material covered but also work on reasoning and math skills. Many teachers have told us that their students really enjoy doing these!

WORD SEARCH PUZZLES
The word search words go in all directions, as indicated on your answer keys. Two of the word search puzzles have the clues listed rather than the words. This makes the puzzle a little more difficult, but it reinforces the material better. Two word search puzzles have words only for students who find the clue puzzles too difficult.

CROSSWORD PUZZLES
Both unit and vocabulary word sections have 4 crossword puzzles.

BINGO CARDS
There are 32 individual bingo cards for the unit words and 32 individual bingo cards for the vocabulary words. You can use your word list as a "call list," calling the words at random and marking them off of your list as you go, or you could use the flash cards by cutting them apart and drawing the words at random from a hat (or box or whatever). To make a better review, you might ask for the definition and spelling of each word as you call it out–or you could call out the definitions and have students tell you the words they need to look for on the puzzle.

JUGGLE LETTERS
The vocabulary juggle letter game is intended to help students learn the spellings of the words. One sheet has the definitions listed on it as an extra help for students who need it or to reinforce the definitions if you choose to do so.

FLASH CARDS
We've included a set of vocabulary flash cards you can duplicate, cut, and fold for your students. Some teachers make a few sets for general use by the class; others make a set for each student. Some teachers duplicate them for each student and have the students cut & fold their own. You can cut out just the words and put them in a hat, have each student pick out one word and write the definition and a sentence for that word. Students then swap words and papers, with the next student adding a sentence of his own under the last one. You can have students swap as many times as you like. Each time the student will read the sentences written prior to his own and then add a sentence. You can cut out the words and definitions separately and play "I Have; Who Has?" Each student in the room draws a word and definition. The first student says, "I have (the name of the word). Who has the definition?" The student with the definition reads it then says, "I have (the name of the vocabulary word she has). Who has the definition?" The round continues until all words and definitions have been given.

Native Son Word List

No.	Word	Clue/Definition
1.	ASHAMED	Bigger feels ___ and resentful when he is with his family.
2.	ASHES	The evidence that leads to Bigger's downfall
3.	BESSIE	Bigger's girlfriend
4.	BIGGER	He murders twice.
5.	BLIND	Mrs. Dalton's handicap
6.	BLUM	Bigger, Gus, Jack and GH plan to rob ___'s Store
7.	BRITTEN	Investigator
8.	BUCKLEY	State prosecutor
9.	BUDDY	Bigger's brother
10.	CELL	Jail room
11.	COURT	Trial room
12.	DALTON	Mr. ___ owns Thomas home; Mary's father
13.	DOC	Owns poolroom
14.	FATE	Book III title
15.	FEAR	Book I title
16.	FLIGHT	Book II title
17.	FURNACE	Where Bigger put Mary's body
18.	GUS	Gang friend of Bigger
19.	HAMMOND	Preacher from Bigger's mother's church
20.	INDIFFERENCE	These were the rhythms of his life: ___ and violence.
21.	JAN	Mary's friend who was a communist
22.	MARY	Rich white girl who is murdered
23.	MAX	Bigger's lawyer
24.	NATIVE	___ Son
25.	OUTSIDE	Half the time I feel like I'm on the ___ of the world peeping in.
26.	PEGGY	Housekeeper
27.	PILLOW	Murder weapon in Mary's murder
28.	PINGPONG	Mr. Dalton sent these tables to the boys' club.
29.	PREJUDICE	Preconceived idea
30.	RANSOM	Bigger plans to get $10,000 from Mr. Dalton as ___ money.
31.	RAPE	Bigger was charged with the ___ and murder of Mary.
32.	SON	Native ___
33.	STOMACH	White folks live right down here in my ___.
34.	VERA	Bigger's sister
35.	WRIGHT	Author Richard

Native Son Fill In The Blanks 1

_____

1. Trial room
2. He murders twice.
3. Bigger was charged with the ___ and murder of Mary.
4. Bigger, Gus, Jack and GH plan to rob ___'s Store
5. Native ___
6. Mrs. Dalton's handicap
7. Bigger's lawyer
8. Jail room
9. Book III title
10. Bigger plans to get $10,000 from Mr. Dalton as ___ money.
11. Preconceived idea
12. Housekeeper
13. Author Richard
14. Rich white girl who is murdered
15. Owns poolroom
16. ___ Son
17. State prosecutor
18. Bigger feels ___ and resentful when he is with his family.
19. These were the rhythms of his life: ___ and violence.
20. Where Bigger put Mary's body

Native Son Fill In The Blanks 1 Answer Key

COURT	1. Trial room
BIGGER	2. He murders twice.
RAPE	3. Bigger was charged with the ___ and murder of Mary.
BLUM	4. Bigger, Gus, Jack and GH plan to rob ___'s Store
SON	5. Native ___
BLIND	6. Mrs. Dalton's handicap
MAX	7. Bigger's lawyer
CELL	8. Jail room
FATE	9. Book III title
RANSOM	10. Bigger plans to get $10,000 from Mr. Dalton as ___ money.
PREJUDICE	11. Preconceived idea
PEGGY	12. Housekeeper
WRIGHT	13. Author Richard
MARY	14. Rich white girl who is murdered
DOC	15. Owns poolroom
NATIVE	16. ___ Son
BUCKLEY	17. State prosecutor
ASHAMED	18. Bigger feels ___ and resentful when he is with his family.
INDIFFERENCE	19. These were the rhythms of his life: ___ and violence.
FURNACE	20. Where Bigger put Mary's body

Native Son Fill In The Blanks 2

1. These were the rhythms of his life: ___ and violence.
2. Preconceived idea
3. Where Bigger put Mary's body
4. Mary's friend who was a communist
5. The evidence that leads to Bigger's downfall
6. Native ___
7. Gang friend of Bigger
8. Mrs. Dalton's handicap
9. Bigger plans to get $10,000 from Mr. Dalton as ___ money.
10. Housekeeper
11. White folks live right down here in my ___.
12. Rich white girl who is murdered
13. Book I title
14. Bigger was charged with the ___ and murder of Mary.
15. Trial room
16. Mr. ___ owns Thomas home; Mary's father
17. Mr. Dalton sent these tables to the boys' club.
18. Preacher from Bigger's mother's church
19. Bigger's girlfriend
20. Bigger's brother

Native Son Fill In The Blanks 2 Answer Key

INDIFFERENCE	1. These were the rhythms of his life: ___ and violence.
PREJUDICE	2. Preconceived idea
FURNACE	3. Where Bigger put Mary's body
JAN	4. Mary's friend who was a communist
ASHES	5. The evidence that leads to Bigger's downfall
SON	6. Native ___
GUS	7. Gang friend of Bigger
BLIND	8. Mrs. Dalton's handicap
RANSOM	9. Bigger plans to get $10,000 from Mr. Dalton as ___ money.
PEGGY	10. Housekeeper
STOMACH	11. White folks live right down here in my ___.
MARY	12. Rich white girl who is murdered
FEAR	13. Book I title
RAPE	14. Bigger was charged with the ___ and murder of Mary.
COURT	15. Trial room
DALTON	16. Mr. ___ owns Thomas home; Mary's father
PINGPONG	17. Mr. Dalton sent these tables to the boys' club.
HAMMOND	18. Preacher from Bigger's mother's church
BESSIE	19. Bigger's girlfriend
BUDDY	20. Bigger's brother

Native Son Fill In The Blanks 3

1. Mrs. Dalton's handicap
2. Bigger's sister
3. Owns poolroom
4. Jail room
5. Murder weapon in Mary's murder
6. Investigator
7. White folks live right down here in my ___.
8. Gang friend of Bigger
9. Mr. ___ owns Thomas home; Mary's father
10. Book III title
11. Book II title
12. Housekeeper
13. ___ Son
14. State prosecutor
15. Bigger's girlfriend
16. He murders twice.
17. Native ___
18. Bigger, Gus, Jack and GH plan to rob ___'s Store
19. Half the time I feel like I'm on the ___ of the world peeping in.
20. Mary's friend who was a communist

Native Son Fill In The Blanks 3 Answer Key

BLIND	1. Mrs. Dalton's handicap
VERA	2. Bigger's sister
DOC	3. Owns poolroom
CELL	4. Jail room
PILLOW	5. Murder weapon in Mary's murder
BRITTEN	6. Investigator
STOMACH	7. White folks live right down here in my ___.
GUS	8. Gang friend of Bigger
DALTON	9. Mr. ___ owns Thomas home; Mary's father
FATE	10. Book III title
FLIGHT	11. Book II title
PEGGY	12. Housekeeper
NATIVE	13. ___ Son
BUCKLEY	14. State prosecutor
BESSIE	15. Bigger's girlfriend
BIGGER	16. He murders twice.
SON	17. Native ___
BLUM	18. Bigger, Gus, Jack and GH plan to rob ___'s Store
OUTSIDE	19. Half the time I feel like I'm on the ___ of the world peeping in.
JAN	20. Mary's friend who was a communist

Native Son Fill In The Blanks 4

1. Gang friend of Bigger
2. Bigger's girlfriend
3. Mrs. Dalton's handicap
4. Author Richard
5. State prosecutor
6. Housekeeper
7. Mr. ___ owns Thomas home; Mary's father
8. Where Bigger put Mary's body
9. Book II title
10. These were the rhythms of his life: ___ and violence.
11. Bigger, Gus, Jack and GH plan to rob ___'s Store
12. Book III title
13. Preconceived idea
14. He murders twice.
15. Rich white girl who is murdered
16. Preacher from Bigger's mother's church
17. Bigger's sister
18. Bigger plans to get $10,000 from Mr. Dalton as ___ money.
19. Bigger's lawyer
20. Half the time I feel like I'm on the ___ of the world peeping in.

Native Son Fill In The Blanks 4 Answer Key

GUS	1. Gang friend of Bigger
BESSIE	2. Bigger's girlfriend
BLIND	3. Mrs. Dalton's handicap
WRIGHT	4. Author Richard
BUCKLEY	5. State prosecutor
PEGGY	6. Housekeeper
DALTON	7. Mr. ___ owns Thomas home; Mary's father
FURNACE	8. Where Bigger put Mary's body
FLIGHT	9. Book II title
INDIFFERENCE	10. These were the rhythms of his life: ___ and violence.
BLUM	11. Bigger, Gus, Jack and GH plan to rob ___'s Store
FATE	12. Book III title
PREJUDICE	13. Preconceived idea
BIGGER	14. He murders twice.
MARY	15. Rich white girl who is murdered
HAMMOND	16. Preacher from Bigger's mother's church
VERA	17. Bigger's sister
RANSOM	18. Bigger plans to get $10,000 from Mr. Dalton as ___ money.
MAX	19. Bigger's lawyer
OUTSIDE	20. Half the time I feel like I'm on the ___ of the world peeping in.

Native Son Matching 1

___ 1. BUCKLEY A. Half the time I feel like I'm on the ___ of the world peeping in.
___ 2. ASHES B. The evidence that leads to Bigger's downfall
___ 3. SON C. Native ___
___ 4. FURNACE D. ___ Son
___ 5. BUDDY E. White folks live right down here in my ___.
___ 6. OUTSIDE F. Bigger was charged with the ___ and murder of Mary.
___ 7. WRIGHT G. State prosecutor
___ 8. NATIVE H. Book III title
___ 9. FATE I. Bigger plans to get $10,000 from Mr. Dalton as ___ money.
___ 10. GUS J. These were the rhythms of his life: ___ and violence.
___ 11. BIGGER K. Investigator
___ 12. COURT L. Bigger's brother
___ 13. VERA M. Gang friend of Bigger
___ 14. BESSIE N. Rich white girl who is murdered
___ 15. RANSOM O. Where Bigger put Mary's body
___ 16. PINGPONG P. Mr. Dalton sent these tables to the boys' club.
___ 17. DALTON Q. He murders twice.
___ 18. RAPE R. Bigger's girlfriend
___ 19. JAN S. Bigger feels ___ and resentful when he is with his family.
___ 20. BRITTEN T. Mr. ___ owns Thomas home; Mary's father
___ 21. INDIFFERENCE U. Mary's friend who was a communist
___ 22. MARY V. Book I title
___ 23. ASHAMED W. Trial room
___ 24. FEAR X. Author Richard
___ 25. STOMACH Y. Bigger's sister

Native Son Matching 1 Answer Key

G - 1. BUCKLEY	A.	Half the time I feel like I'm on the ___ of the world peeping in.
B - 2. ASHES	B.	The evidence that leads to Bigger's downfall
C - 3. SON	C.	Native ___
O - 4. FURNACE	D.	___ Son
L - 5. BUDDY	E.	White folks live right down here in my ___.
A - 6. OUTSIDE	F.	Bigger was charged with the ___ and murder of Mary.
X - 7. WRIGHT	G.	State prosecutor
D - 8. NATIVE	H.	Book III title
H - 9. FATE	I.	Bigger plans to get $10,000 from Mr. Dalton as ___ money.
M - 10. GUS	J.	These were the rhythms of his life: ___ and violence.
Q - 11. BIGGER	K.	Investigator
W - 12. COURT	L.	Bigger's brother
Y - 13. VERA	M.	Gang friend of Bigger
R - 14. BESSIE	N.	Rich white girl who is murdered
I - 15. RANSOM	O.	Where Bigger put Mary's body
P - 16. PINGPONG	P.	Mr. Dalton sent these tables to the boys' club.
T - 17. DALTON	Q.	He murders twice.
F - 18. RAPE	R.	Bigger's girlfriend
U - 19. JAN	S.	Bigger feels ___ and resentful when he is with his family.
K - 20. BRITTEN	T.	Mr. ___ owns Thomas home; Mary's father
J - 21. INDIFFERENCE	U.	Mary's friend who was a communist
N - 22. MARY	V.	Book I title
S - 23. ASHAMED	W.	Trial room
V - 24. FEAR	X.	Author Richard
E - 25. STOMACH	Y.	Bigger's sister

Native Son Matching 2

___ 1. BLUM   A. ___ Son
___ 2. BESSIE   B. The evidence that leads to Bigger's downfall
___ 3. VERA   C. Bigger was charged with the ___ and murder of Mary.
___ 4. MARY   D. Mary's friend who was a communist
___ 5. INDIFFERENCE   E. Bigger's girlfriend
___ 6. DALTON   F. State prosecutor
___ 7. MAX   G. Book II title
___ 8. JAN   H. Book I title
___ 9. WRIGHT   I. Bigger's sister
___ 10. RAPE   J. Mrs. Dalton's handicap
___ 11. BUCKLEY   K. White folks live right down here in my ___.
___ 12. STOMACH   L. Bigger, Gus, Jack and GH plan to rob ___'s Store
___ 13. FLIGHT   M. Trial room
___ 14. ASHES   N. Rich white girl who is murdered
___ 15. BLIND   O. These were the rhythms of his life: ___ and violence.
___ 16. OUTSIDE   P. Mr. ___ owns Thomas home; Mary's father
___ 17. COURT   Q. Author Richard
___ 18. PREJUDICE   R. Book III title
___ 19. NATIVE   S. Investigator
___ 20. PINGPONG   T. Preconceived idea
___ 21. FEAR   U. Bigger's lawyer
___ 22. GUS   V. Preacher from Bigger's mother's church
___ 23. BRITTEN   W. Mr. Dalton sent these tables to the boys' club.
___ 24. FATE   X. Half the time I feel like I'm on the ___ of the world peeping in.
___ 25. HAMMOND   Y. Gang friend of Bigger

Native Son Matching 2 Answer Key

L - 1. BLUM		A. ___ Son
E - 2. BESSIE		B. The evidence that leads to Bigger's downfall
I - 3. VERA		C. Bigger was charged with the ___ and murder of Mary.
N - 4. MARY		D. Mary's friend who was a communist
O - 5. INDIFFERENCE		E. Bigger's girlfriend
P - 6. DALTON		F. State prosecutor
U - 7. MAX		G. Book II title
D - 8. JAN		H. Book I title
Q - 9. WRIGHT		I. Bigger's sister
C - 10. RAPE		J. Mrs. Dalton's handicap
F - 11. BUCKLEY		K. White folks live right down here in my ___.
K - 12. STOMACH		L. Bigger, Gus, Jack and GH plan to rob ___'s Store
G - 13. FLIGHT		M. Trial room
B - 14. ASHES		N. Rich white girl who is murdered
J - 15. BLIND		O. These were the rhythms of his life: ___ and violence.
X - 16. OUTSIDE		P. Mr. ___ owns Thomas home; Mary's father
M - 17. COURT		Q. Author Richard
T - 18. PREJUDICE		R. Book III title
A - 19. NATIVE		S. Investigator
W - 20. PINGPONG		T. Preconceived idea
H - 21. FEAR		U. Bigger's lawyer
Y - 22. GUS		V. Preacher from Bigger's mother's church
S - 23. BRITTEN		W. Mr. Dalton sent these tables to the boys' club.
R - 24. FATE		X. Half the time I feel like I'm on the ___ of the world peeping in.
V - 25. HAMMOND		Y. Gang friend of Bigger

Native Son Matching 3

___ 1. DOC A. Investigator
___ 2. BUCKLEY B. Bigger's brother
___ 3. BUDDY C. Where Bigger put Mary's body
___ 4. PREJUDICE D. Bigger's sister
___ 5. ASHAMED E. Rich white girl who is murdered
___ 6. DALTON F. Book I title
___ 7. MAX G. Preconceived idea
___ 8. FATE H. Bigger's lawyer
___ 9. VERA I. Owns poolroom
___10. BESSIE J. Mrs. Dalton's handicap
___11. SON K. Book III title
___12. FLIGHT L. Mary's friend who was a communist
___13. BRITTEN M. These were the rhythms of his life: ___ and violence.
___14. RAPE N. Mr. ___ owns Thomas home; Mary's father
___15. PEGGY O. Housekeeper
___16. MARY P. Author Richard
___17. WRIGHT Q. Native ___
___18. HAMMOND R. White folks live right down here in my ___.
___19. JAN S. Bigger, Gus, Jack and GH plan to rob ___'s Store
___20. INDIFFERENCE T. Bigger feels ___ and resentful when he is with his family.
___21. FURNACE U. Bigger's girlfriend
___22. BLUM V. Preacher from Bigger's mother's church
___23. FEAR W. Book II title
___24. BLIND X. State prosecutor
___25. STOMACH Y. Bigger was charged with the ___ and murder of Mary.

Native Son Matching 3 Answer Key

I - 1. DOC		A. Investigator
X - 2. BUCKLEY		B. Bigger's brother
B - 3. BUDDY		C. Where Bigger put Mary's body
G - 4. PREJUDICE		D. Bigger's sister
T - 5. ASHAMED		E. Rich white girl who is murdered
N - 6. DALTON		F. Book I title
H - 7. MAX		G. Preconceived idea
K - 8. FATE		H. Bigger's lawyer
D - 9. VERA		I. Owns poolroom
U - 10. BESSIE		J. Mrs. Dalton's handicap
Q - 11. SON		K. Book III title
W - 12. FLIGHT		L. Mary's friend who was a communist
A - 13. BRITTEN		M. These were the rhythms of his life: ___ and violence.
Y - 14. RAPE		N. Mr. ___ owns Thomas home; Mary's father
O - 15. PEGGY		O. Housekeeper
E - 16. MARY		P. Author Richard
P - 17. WRIGHT		Q. Native ___
V - 18. HAMMOND		R. White folks live right down here in my ___.
L - 19. JAN		S. Bigger, Gus, Jack and GH plan to rob ___'s Store
M - 20. INDIFFERENCE		T. Bigger feels ___ and resentful when he is with his family.
C - 21. FURNACE		U. Bigger's girlfriend
S - 22. BLUM		V. Preacher from Bigger's mother's church
F - 23. FEAR		W. Book II title
J - 24. BLIND		X. State prosecutor
R - 25. STOMACH		Y. Bigger was charged with the ___ and murder of Mary.

Copyrighted

Native Son Matching 4

___ 1. INDIFFERENCE		A. Author Richard
___ 2. SON			B. Book II title
___ 3. PEGGY			C. Bigger, Gus, Jack and GH plan to rob ___'s Store
___ 4. FURNACE			D. Preacher from Bigger's mother's church
___ 5. RANSOM			E. He murders twice.
___ 6. COURT			F. Mrs. Dalton's handicap
___ 7. BRITTEN			G. Bigger's brother
___ 8. GUS			H. Bigger plans to get $10,000 from Mr. Dalton as ___ money.
___ 9. HAMMOND			I. Owns poolroom
___10. BIGGER			J. Bigger's lawyer
___11. MARY			K. These were the rhythms of his life: ___ and violence.
___12. MAX			L. Bigger was charged with the ___ and murder of Mary.
___13. JAN			M. Investigator
___14. BLUM			N. Mr. Dalton sent these tables to the boys' club.
___15. DOC			O. Rich white girl who is murdered
___16. RAPE			P. Trial room
___17. ASHAMED			Q. Housekeeper
___18. CELL			R. Mary's friend who was a communist
___19. BUCKLEY			S. Bigger feels ___ and resentful when he is with his family.
___20. FLIGHT			T. State prosecutor
___21. NATIVE			U. Gang friend of Bigger
___22. BLIND			V. Native ___
___23. WRIGHT			W. Jail room
___24. BUDDY			X. Where Bigger put Mary's body
___25. PINGPONG			Y. ___ Son

Native Son Matching 4 Answer Key

K - 1. INDIFFERENCE	A.	Author Richard
V - 2. SON	B.	Book II title
Q - 3. PEGGY	C.	Bigger, Gus, Jack and GH plan to rob ___'s Store
X - 4. FURNACE	D.	Preacher from Bigger's mother's church
H - 5. RANSOM	E.	He murders twice.
P - 6. COURT	F.	Mrs. Dalton's handicap
M - 7. BRITTEN	G.	Bigger's brother
U - 8. GUS	H.	Bigger plans to get $10,000 from Mr. Dalton as ___ money.
D - 9. HAMMOND	I.	Owns poolroom
E - 10. BIGGER	J.	Bigger's lawyer
O - 11. MARY	K.	These were the rhythms of his life: ___ and violence.
J - 12. MAX	L.	Bigger was charged with the ___ and murder of Mary.
R - 13. JAN	M.	Investigator
C - 14. BLUM	N.	Mr. Dalton sent these tables to the boys' club.
I - 15. DOC	O.	Rich white girl who is murdered
L - 16. RAPE	P.	Trial room
S - 17. ASHAMED	Q.	Housekeeper
W - 18. CELL	R.	Mary's friend who was a communist
T - 19. BUCKLEY	S.	Bigger feels ___ and resentful when he is with his family.
B - 20. FLIGHT	T.	State prosecutor
Y - 21. NATIVE	U.	Gang friend of Bigger
F - 22. BLIND	V.	Native ___
A - 23. WRIGHT	W.	Jail room
G - 24. BUDDY	X.	Where Bigger put Mary's body
N - 25. PINGPONG	Y.	___ Son

Native Son Magic Squares 1

Match the definition with the vocabulary word. Put your answers in the magic squares below. When your answers are correct, all columns and rows will add to the same number.

A. BUDDY
B. RAPE
C. BESSIE
D. WRIGHT
E. MARY
F. STOMACH
G. HAMMOND
H. PILLOW
I. SON
J. JAN
K. FURNACE
L. FLIGHT
M. BLUM
N. COURT
O. FEAR
P. VERA

1. Book I title
2. Author Richard
3. Mary's friend who was a communist
4. Rich white girl who is murdered
5. Native ___
6. White folks live right down here in my ___.
7. Bigger's sister
8. Bigger's girlfriend
9. Murder weapon in Mary's murder
10. Where Bigger put Mary's body
11. Bigger's brother
12. Trial room
13. Bigger was charged with the ___ and murder of Mary.
14. Bigger, Gus, Jack and GH plan to rob ___'s Store
15. Preacher from Bigger's mother's church
16. Book II title

A=	B=	C=	D=
E=	F=	G=	H=
I=	J=	K=	L=
M=	N=	O=	P=

Native Son Magic Squares 1 Answer Key

Match the definition with the vocabulary word. Put your answers in the magic squares below. When your answers are correct, all columns and rows will add to the same number.

A. BUDDY
B. RAPE
C. BESSIE
D. WRIGHT
E. MARY
F. STOMACH
G. HAMMOND
H. PILLOW
I. SON
J. JAN
K. FURNACE
L. FLIGHT
M. BLUM
N. COURT
O. FEAR
P. VERA

1. Book I title
2. Author Richard
3. Mary's friend who was a communist
4. Rich white girl who is murdered
5. Native ___
6. White folks live right down here in my ___.
7. Bigger's sister
8. Bigger's girlfriend
9. Murder weapon in Mary's murder
10. Where Bigger put Mary's body
11. Bigger's brother
12. Trial room
13. Bigger was charged with the ___ and murder of Mary.
14. Bigger, Gus, Jack and GH plan to rob ___'s Store
15. Preacher from Bigger's mother's church
16. Book II title

A=11	B=13	C=8	D=2
E=4	F=6	G=15	H=9
I=5	J=3	K=10	L=16
M=14	N=12	O=1	P=7

Native Son Magic Squares 2

Match the definition with the vocabulary word. Put your answers in the magic squares below. When your answers are correct, all columns and rows will add to the same number.

A. BLUM
B. OUTSIDE
C. JAN
D. COURT
E. HAMMOND
F. PREJUDICE
G. BIGGER
H. RAPE
I. BRITTEN
J. STOMACH
K. PINGPONG
L. ASHAMED
M. BUDDY
N. DOC
O. BLIND
P. SON

1. Mary's friend who was a communist
2. White folks live right down here in my ___.
3. Preconceived idea
4. Mrs. Dalton's handicap
5. Native ___
6. Preacher from Bigger's mother's church
7. Investigator
8. Trial room
9. Bigger's brother
10. Bigger was charged with the ___ and murder of Mary.
11. Bigger feels ___ and resentful when he is with his family.
12. Bigger, Gus, Jack and GH plan to rob ___'s Store
13. Half the time I feel like I'm on the ___ of the world peeping in.
14. Mr. Dalton sent these tables to the boys' club.
15. He murders twice.
16. Owns poolroom

A=	B=	C=	D=
E=	F=	G=	H=
I=	J=	K=	L=
M=	N=	O=	P=

Native Son Magic Squares 2 Answer Key

Match the definition with the vocabulary word. Put your answers in the magic squares below. When your answers are correct, all columns and rows will add to the same number.

A. BLUM
B. OUTSIDE
C. JAN
D. COURT
E. HAMMOND
F. PREJUDICE
G. BIGGER
H. RAPE
I. BRITTEN
J. STOMACH
K. PINGPONG
L. ASHAMED
M. BUDDY
N. DOC
O. BLIND
P. SON

1. Mary's friend who was a communist
2. White folks live right down here in my ___.
3. Preconceived idea
4. Mrs. Dalton's handicap
5. Native ___
6. Preacher from Bigger's mother's church
7. Investigator
8. Trial room
9. Bigger's brother
10. Bigger was charged with the ___ and murder of Mary.
11. Bigger feels ___ and resentful when he is with his family.
12. Bigger, Gus, Jack and GH plan to rob ___'s Store
13. Half the time I feel like I'm on the ___ of the world peeping in.
14. Mr. Dalton sent these tables to the boys' club.
15. He murders twice.
16. Owns poolroom

A=12	B=13	C=1	D=8
E=6	F=3	G=15	H=10
I=7	J=2	K=14	L=11
M=9	N=16	O=4	P=5

Native Son Magic Squares 3

Match the definition with the vocabulary word. Put your answers in the magic squares below. When your answers are correct, all columns and rows will add to the same number.

A. PILLOW
B. FATE
C. DOC
D. RANSOM
E. MARY
F. FLIGHT
G. FEAR
H. BLIND
I. JAN
J. COURT
K. CELL
L. BRITTEN
M. PEGGY
N. INDIFFERENCE
O. STOMACH
P. WRIGHT

1. Book II title
2. Mary's friend who was a communist
3. White folks live right down here in my ___.
4. Bigger plans to get $10,000 from Mr. Dalton as ___ money.
5. Housekeeper
6. Book III title
7. Mrs. Dalton's handicap
8. Jail room
9. Owns poolroom
10. Author Richard
11. Trial room
12. Rich white girl who is murdered
13. Investigator
14. Book I title
15. Murder weapon in Mary's murder
16. These were the rhythms of his life: ___ and violence.

A=	B=	C=	D=
E=	F=	G=	H=
I=	J=	K=	L=
M=	N=	O=	P=

Native Son Magic Squares 3 Answer Key

Match the definition with the vocabulary word. Put your answers in the magic squares below. When your answers are correct, all columns and rows will add to the same number.

A. PILLOW
B. FATE
C. DOC
D. RANSOM
E. MARY
F. FLIGHT
G. FEAR
H. BLIND
I. JAN
J. COURT
K. CELL
L. BRITTEN
M. PEGGY
N. INDIFFERENCE
O. STOMACH
P. WRIGHT

1. Book II title
2. Mary's friend who was a communist
3. White folks live right down here in my ___.
4. Bigger plans to get $10,000 from Mr. Dalton as ___ money.
5. Housekeeper
6. Book III title
7. Mrs. Dalton's handicap
8. Jail room
9. Owns poolroom
10. Author Richard
11. Trial room
12. Rich white girl who is murdered
13. Investigator
14. Book I title
15. Murder weapon in Mary's murder
16. These were the rhythms of his life: ___ and violence.

A=15	B=6	C=9	D=4
E=12	F=1	G=14	H=7
I=2	J=11	K=8	L=13
M=5	N=16	O=3	P=10

Native Son Magic Squares 4

Match the definition with the vocabulary word. Put your answers in the magic squares below. When your answers are correct, all columns and rows will add to the same number.

A. STOMACH
B. FLIGHT
C. JAN
D. ASHES
E. BLUM
F. DALTON
G. BESSIE
H. PEGGY
I. VERA
J. FURNACE
K. FEAR
L. HAMMOND
M. MAX
N. OUTSIDE
O. WRIGHT
P. INDIFFERENCE

1. Book II title
2. Bigger's girlfriend
3. Book I title
4. Half the time I feel like I'm on the ___ of the world peeping in.
5. Bigger's lawyer
6. Preacher from Bigger's mother's church
7. Housekeeper
8. White folks live right down here in my ___.
9. These were the rhythms of his life: ___ and violence.
10. Bigger's sister
11. Bigger, Gus, Jack and GH plan to rob ___'s Store
12. The evidence that leads to Bigger's downfall
13. Mary's friend who was a communist
14. Mr. ___ owns Thomas home; Mary's father
15. Where Bigger put Mary's body
16. Author Richard

A=	B=	C=	D=
E=	F=	G=	H=
I=	J=	K=	L=
M=	N=	O=	P=

Native Son Magic Squares 4 Answer Key

Match the definition with the vocabulary word. Put your answers in the magic squares below. When your answers are correct, all columns and rows will add to the same number.

A. STOMACH
B. FLIGHT
C. JAN
D. ASHES
E. BLUM
F. DALTON
G. BESSIE
H. PEGGY
I. VERA
J. FURNACE
K. FEAR
L. HAMMOND
M. MAX
N. OUTSIDE
O. WRIGHT
P. INDIFFERENCE

1. Book II title
2. Bigger's girlfriend
3. Book I title
4. Half the time I feel like I'm on the ___ of the world peeping in.
5. Bigger's lawyer
6. Preacher from Bigger's mother's church
7. Housekeeper
8. White folks live right down here in my ___.
9. These were the rhythms of his life: ___ and violence.
10. Bigger's sister
11. Bigger, Gus, Jack and GH plan to rob ___'s Store
12. The evidence that leads to Bigger's downfall
13. Mary's friend who was a communist
14. Mr. ___ owns Thomas home; Mary's father
15. Where Bigger put Mary's body
16. Author Richard

A=8	B=1	C=13	D=12
E=11	F=14	G=2	H=7
I=10	J=15	K=3	L=6
M=5	N=4	O=16	P=9

Native Son Word Search 1

```
P I N G P O N G Y B O U T S I D E J M
F S W Z Y H A Z X C U S B N W C R C L
Y R W B H N T L H T M C D K A S N Y E
B X W Y D P I S B Z N I K N K X F C N
W E Y B B N V N D V F J R L D C I N Z
Z K S C Z P E R C F L U J L E D H Y B
Y J P S Q Z Q D E D F D P R U Y J G R
N P M Y I W B R S G Z C S J V J K N Z
S K R W T E E F Y T F W E F H Q B L P
P M N N Y N Z T M A O R K W B I C Y V
H H J Q C D N H H S P M R D G L O G M
X Q L E H P M G S H P Z A G A S U G K
W N C P L Z M I F A L S E C U L R E X
Q O C E L L B L U M W R I G H T P V
D D W P D D M F O E A C Y A N A I O M
X L H W D R Q S F D R X M E F L P G N
N G Q N M W N L K G Q M T T L N H F V
R M I L S A R A P E O T V O K S E X L
P L J N R C R V Y N I Q W E V A O W F
B F D Z F M G Y D R Y M X B R D J N Y
A S H E S P F P B U D D Y K J A N G M
```

Author Richard (6)
Bigger feels ___ and resentful when he is with his family. (7)
Bigger plans to get $10,000 from Mr. Dalton as ___ money. (6)
Bigger was charged with the ___ and murder of Mary. (4)
Bigger's brother (5)
Bigger's girlfriend (6)
Bigger's lawyer (3)
Bigger's sister (4)
Bigger, Gus, Jack and GH plan to rob ___'s Store (4)
Book I title (4)
Book II title (6)
Book III title (4)
Gang friend of Bigger (3)
Half the time I feel like I'm on the ___ of the world peeping in. (7)
He murders twice. (6)
Housekeeper (5)
Investigator (7)
Jail room (4)

Mary's friend who was a communist (3)
Mr. Dalton sent these tables to the boys' club. (8)
Mr. ___ owns Thomas home; Mary's father (6)
Mrs. Dalton's handicap (5)
Murder weapon in Mary's murder (6)
Native ___ (3)
Owns poolroom (3)
Preacher from Bigger's mother's church (7)
Preconceived idea (9)
Rich white girl who is murdered (4)
State prosecutor (7)
The evidence that leads to Bigger's downfall (5)
These were the rhythms of his life: ___ and violence. (12)
Trial room (5)
Where Bigger put Mary's body (7)
White folks live right down here in my ___. (7)
___ Son (6)

Native Son Word Search 1 Answer Key

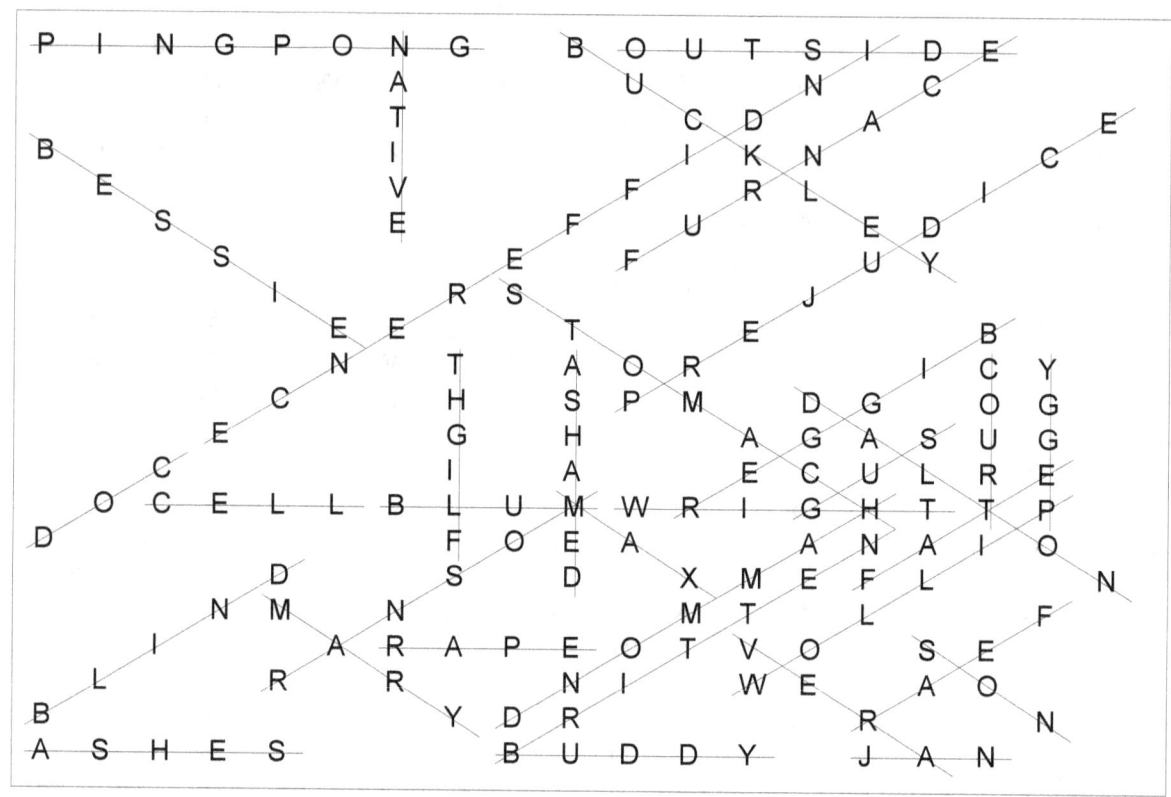

Author Richard (6)
Bigger feels ___ and resentful when he is with his family. (7)
Bigger plans to get $10,000 from Mr. Dalton as ___ money. (6)
Bigger was charged with the ___ and murder of Mary. (4)
Bigger's brother (5)
Bigger's girlfriend (6)
Bigger's lawyer (3)
Bigger's sister (4)
Bigger, Gus, Jack and GH plan to rob ___'s Store (4)
Book I title (4)
Book II title (6)
Book III title (4)
Gang friend of Bigger (3)
Half the time I feel like I'm on the ___ of the world peeping in. (7)
He murders twice. (6)
Housekeeper (5)
Investigator (7)
Jail room (4)

Mary's friend who was a communist (3)
Mr. Dalton sent these tables to the boys' club. (8)
Mr. ___ owns Thomas home; Mary's father (6)
Mrs. Dalton's handicap (5)
Murder weapon in Mary's murder (6)
Native ___ (3)
Owns poolroom (3)
Preacher from Bigger's mother's church (7)
Preconceived idea (9)
Rich white girl who is murdered (4)
State prosecutor (7)
The evidence that leads to Bigger's downfall (5)
These were the rhythms of his life: ___ and violence. (12)
Trial room (5)
Where Bigger put Mary's body (7)
White folks live right down here in my ___. (7)
___ Son (6)

Native Son Word Search 2

```
D N O M M A H T T C B P I L L O W A Y
A F F A H X H H F O R S P W S Y I S B
L U L R B G X G A U I J W X L N N H M
T R V Y I M W I T R T K M W F R D A T
O N H R J S D L E T T A F E A R I M G
N A W J U P Y F Z G E M S S P B F E Z
G C Z G Y R R D B S N S J H G K F D V
J E G X C E Z M M C H W V Y E D E C G
C E L L B J B E S S I E S Y R S R F B
H T M L X U Y K W L J P E V G W E J C
P K K Y G D X S D X P L Z K C P N S F
D H X X Z I Z X M Y K D P R V I C N Q
B X S J F C W S G C T S P Q C N E Q V
G W C X J E M G U K F T P Y C G G G D
N G W M R N E B T H J W V G F P F K H
P N X S G P J R C X J D S T P O T R J
J Y A N C H D A Q V Y H B Q D N E C S
F Y Q T S V M N P B D L W N Y G V E N
V V G N I O M S B X D P I N G D P Y R
R B X O T V M O A R U L A I C A O R G
O U T S I D E M U L B J B A R E V C N
```

Author Richard (6)
Bigger feels ___ and resentful when he is with his family. (7)
Bigger plans to get $10,000 from Mr. Dalton as ___ money. (6)
Bigger was charged with the ___ and murder of Mary. (4)
Bigger's brother (5)
Bigger's girlfriend (6)
Bigger's lawyer (3)
Bigger's sister (4)
Bigger, Gus, Jack and GH plan to rob ___'s Store (4)
Book I title (4)
Book II title (6)
Book III title (4)
Gang friend of Bigger (3)
Half the time I feel like I'm on the ___ of the world peeping in. (7)
He murders twice. (6)
Housekeeper (5)
Investigator (7)
Jail room (4)
Mary's friend who was a communist (3)
Mr. Dalton sent these tables to the boys' club. (8)
Mr. ___ owns Thomas home; Mary's father (6)
Mrs. Dalton's handicap (5)
Murder weapon in Mary's murder (6)
Native ___ (3)
Owns poolroom (3)
Preacher from Bigger's mother's church (7)
Preconceived idea (9)
Rich white girl who is murdered (4)
State prosecutor (7)
The evidence that leads to Bigger's downfall (5)
These were the rhythms of his life: ___ and violence. (12)
Trial room (5)
Where Bigger put Mary's body (7)
White folks live right down here in my ___. (7)
___ Son (6)

Native Son Word Search 2 Answer Key

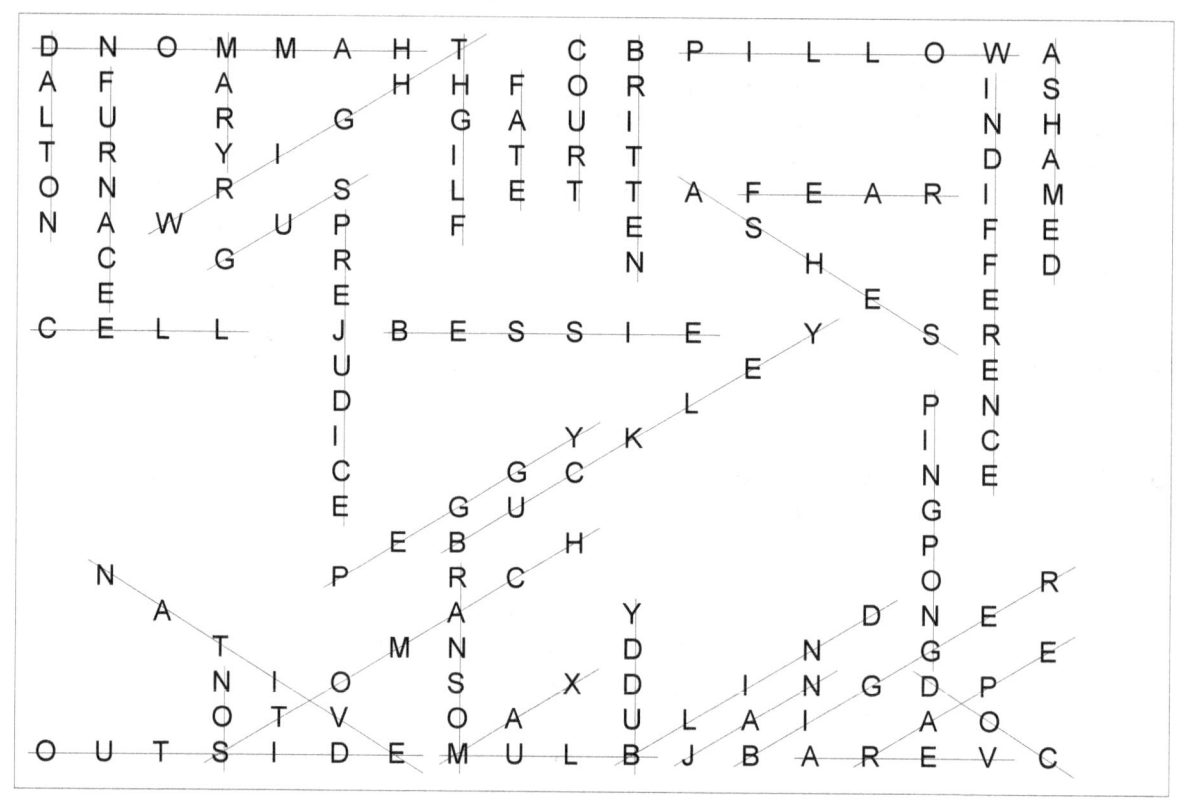

Author Richard (6)
Bigger feels ___ and resentful when he is with his family. (7)
Bigger plans to get $10,000 from Mr. Dalton as ___ money. (6)
Bigger was charged with the ___ and murder of Mary. (4)
Bigger's brother (5)
Bigger's girlfriend (6)
Bigger's lawyer (3)
Bigger's sister (4)
Bigger, Gus, Jack and GH plan to rob ___'s Store (4)
Book I title (4)
Book II title (6)
Book III title (4)
Gang friend of Bigger (3)
Half the time I feel like I'm on the ___ of the world peeping in. (7)
He murders twice. (6)
Housekeeper (5)
Investigator (7)
Jail room (4)

Mary's friend who was a communist (3)
Mr. Dalton sent these tables to the boys' club. (8)
Mr. ___ owns Thomas home; Mary's father (6)
Mrs. Dalton's handicap (5)
Murder weapon in Mary's murder (6)
Native ___ (3)
Owns poolroom (3)
Preacher from Bigger's mother's church (7)
Preconceived idea (9)
Rich white girl who is murdered (4)
State prosecutor (7)
The evidence that leads to Bigger's downfall (5)
These were the rhythms of his life: ___ and violence. (12)
Trial room (5)
Where Bigger put Mary's body (7)
White folks live right down here in my ___. (7)
___ Son (6)

Native Son Word Search 3

```
B W Z B H M O P A S H A M E D V E R A
I F S U K A Q U E H T H C P G K F N Q
G K M D N R B H T D J O H W E S P Q F
G W Q D M Y S R P S K B M D M G H G G
E J R Y K A R X I R I R W A X T G G T
R Y T I N R V F F T E D B N C B K Y P
X N C G G B Q Y U K T J E F Z H N D W
K C Q K K H V T R S W E U C N M M B X
G T D Z F N T X N X N H N D P B Q D G
G P G Q B H Z R A G J S D M I H T C S
T K D B G G Q Y C S V B R Z F C S K H
I N D I F F E R E N C E P X Y B E R T
R R G F Y C F Y C E S W R T V V Y V N
H H H W H N L Q P V D F H R G J R M K
X P G D D L I Z F I A P I N G P O N G
E G P G F P G J P T L V X E L S M S W
I Z P W V A H V A A T C A P N S U O C
S K C O U R T C D N O M M A H S L N F
S F R B V W S E E D N Q R R U L B R M
E V R S R K Y B C L F H H G I P F S R
B L I N D T B U C K L E Y P F E A R T
```

ASHAMED	CELL	HAMMOND	PINGPONG
ASHES	COURT	INDIFFERENCE	PREJUDICE
BESSIE	DALTON	JAN	RANSOM
BIGGER	DOC	MARY	RAPE
BLIND	FATE	MAX	SON
BLUM	FEAR	NATIVE	STOMACH
BRITTEN	FLIGHT	OUTSIDE	VERA
BUCKLEY	FURNACE	PEGGY	WRIGHT
BUDDY	GUS	PILLOW	

Native Son Word Search 3 Answer Key

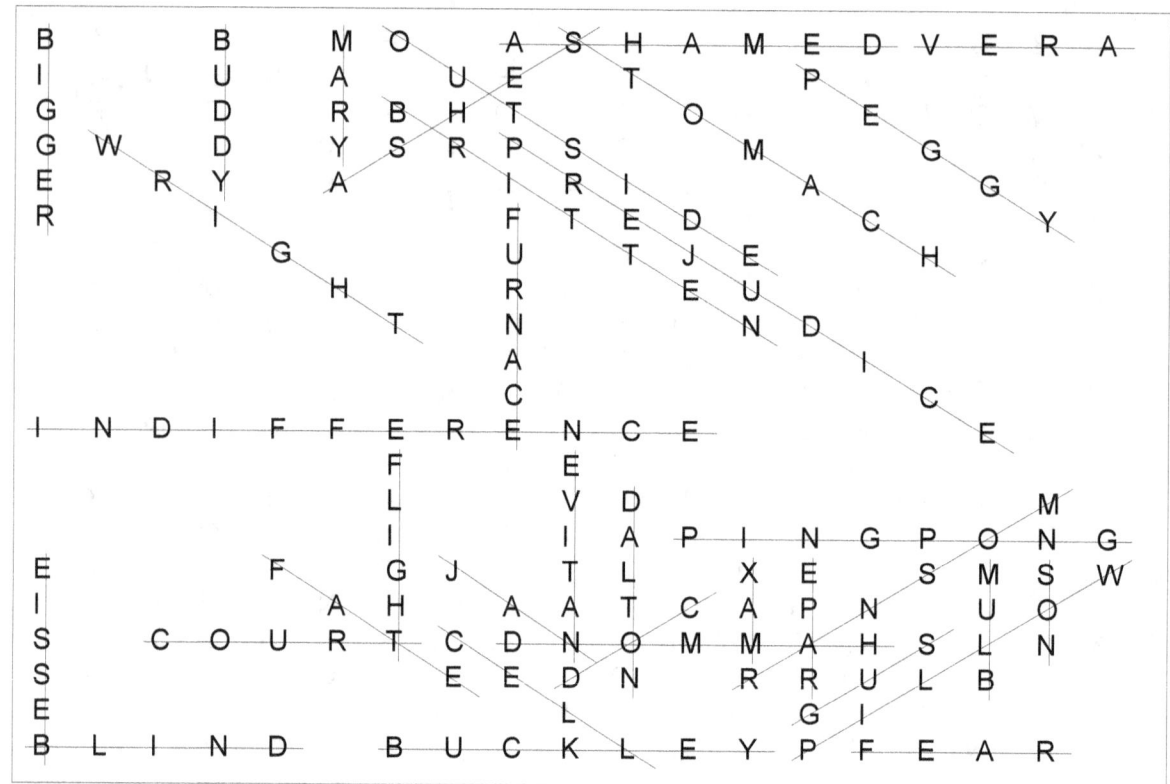

ASHAMED	CELL	HAMMOND	PINGPONG
ASHES	COURT	INDIFFERENCE	PREJUDICE
BESSIE	DALTON	JAN	RANSOM
BIGGER	DOC	MARY	RAPE
BLIND	FATE	MAX	SON
BLUM	FEAR	NATIVE	STOMACH
BRITTEN	FLIGHT	OUTSIDE	VERA
BUCKLEY	FURNACE	PEGGY	WRIGHT
BUDDY	GUS	PILLOW	

Native Son Word Search 4

```
P R E J U D I C E S D C O U R T R F V
I I P A F M T X U O N O L M A H A U C
N W L N Z A C G B N O M C T N G P R Y
G B R L B K T F L X M K A B S I E N G
P D Y I O U L E U M M S S X O L C A Y
O V X M G W D V M X A R H T M F N C Q
N F E V P H T D N N H S E S D D E E C
G X E R C Z T E Y O U T S I D E R P L
W R F A A V T I P J B O M H H N E D T
L B Z S R T R S T R Q M D S J G F X H
M B S T I T C S Q M Z A L A G T F G P
M H B R L B C E S J Z C S Y Y H I B Y
V L B C D Q G B T R X H J L B H D I W
J J Z X M Y C L V W A L T Y U W N G D
V V L N W N L I N M M V J M C M I G C
G F B P D D G N E H K E C T K L A E F
V V F Z P S T D R G V N O T L A D R V
N H W L K K N B G I L F D L E T S P Y
L Q H G Y R D N T M N D E B Y Z K L T
T V X B Y Y P A X V T C K V V P W J N
G H H B L J N J Q R B V D S J P K C K
```

ASHAMED	CELL	HAMMOND	PINGPONG
ASHES	COURT	INDIFFERENCE	PREJUDICE
BESSIE	DALTON	JAN	RANSOM
BIGGER	DOC	MARY	RAPE
BLIND	FATE	MAX	SON
BLUM	FEAR	NATIVE	STOMACH
BRITTEN	FLIGHT	OUTSIDE	VERA
BUCKLEY	FURNACE	PEGGY	WRIGHT
BUDDY	GUS	PILLOW	

Native Son Word Search 4 Answer Key

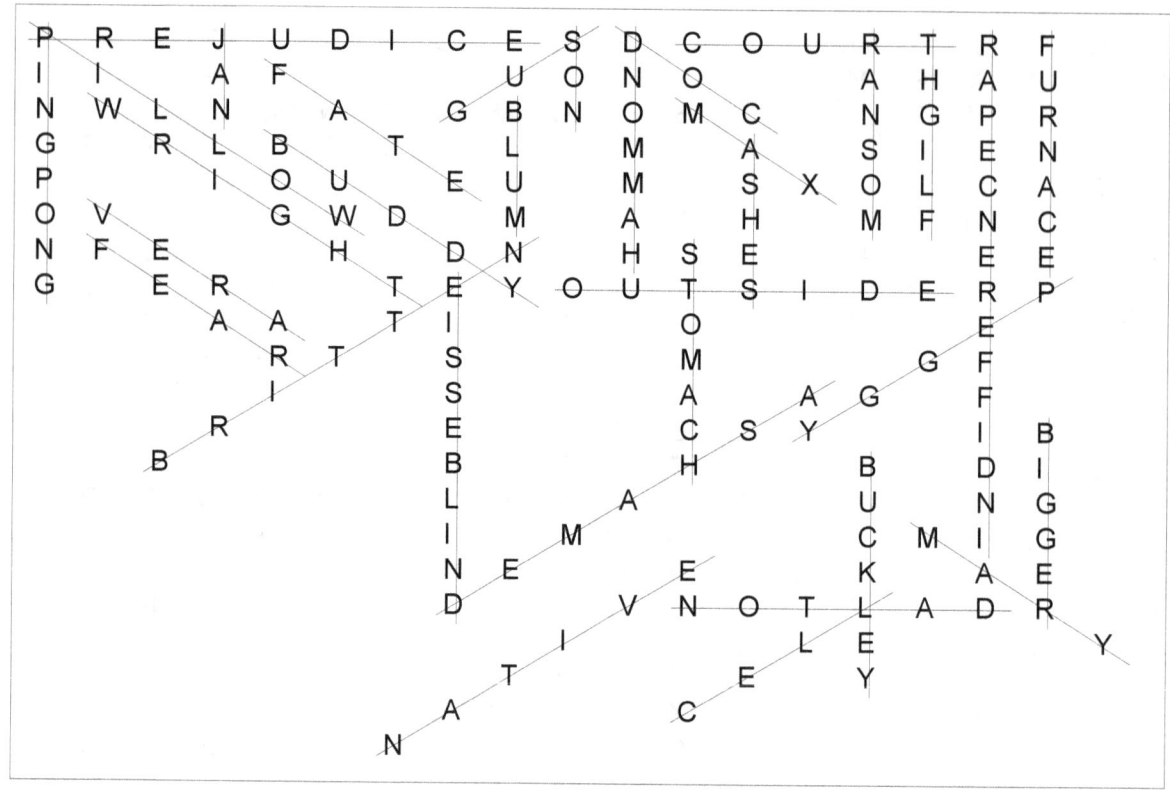

ASHAMED	CELL	HAMMOND	PINGPONG
ASHES	COURT	INDIFFERENCE	PREJUDICE
BESSIE	DALTON	JAN	RANSOM
BIGGER	DOC	MARY	RAPE
BLIND	FATE	MAX	SON
BLUM	FEAR	NATIVE	STOMACH
BRITTEN	FLIGHT	OUTSIDE	VERA
BUCKLEY	FURNACE	PEGGY	WRIGHT
BUDDY	GUS	PILLOW	

Native Son Crossword 1

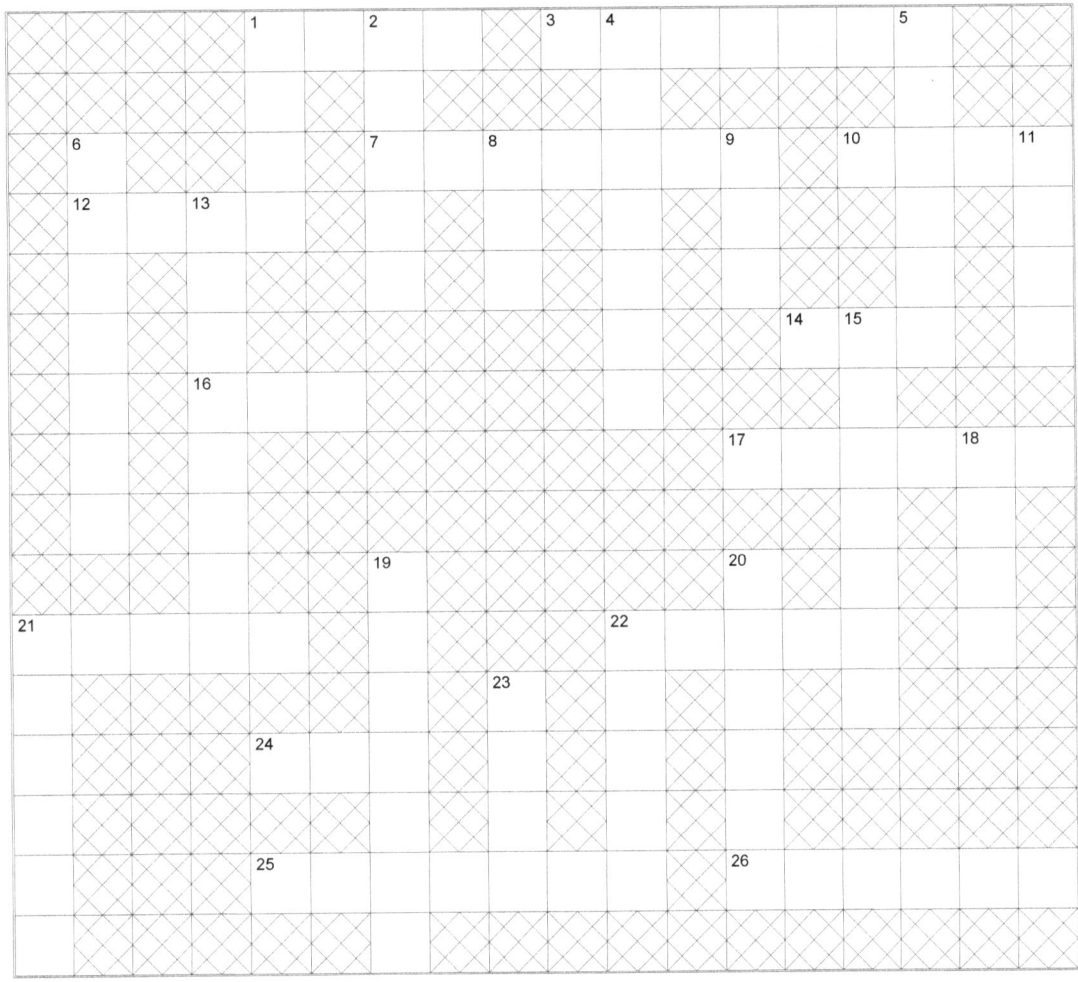

Across
1. Book I title
3. Bigger feels ___ and resentful when he is with his family.
7. Preacher from Bigger's mother's church
10. Bigger, Gus, Jack and GH plan to rob ___'s Store
12. Bigger was charged with the ___ and murder of Mary.
14. Native ___
16. Gang friend of Bigger
17. ___ Son
21. Housekeeper
22. Mrs. Dalton's handicap
24. Mary's friend who was a communist
25. State prosecutor
26. Bigger plans to get $10,000 from Mr. Dalton as ___ money.

Down
1. Book III title
2. The evidence that leads to Bigger's downfall
4. White folks live right down here in my ___.
5. Mr. ___ owns Thomas home; Mary's father
6. Investigator
8. Bigger's lawyer
9. Owns poolroom
11. Rich white girl who is murdered
13. Mr. Dalton sent these tables to the boys' club.
15. Half the time I feel like I'm on the ___ of the world peeping in.
18. Bigger's sister
19. Where Bigger put Mary's body
20. He murders twice.
21. Murder weapon in Mary's murder
22. Bigger's brother
23. Jail room

Native Son Crossword 1 Answer Key

		1 F	E	2 A	R		3 A	4 S	H	A	M	E	5 D	
		A		S				T					A	
	6 B	T		7 H	A	8 M	M	O	N	9 D	10 B	L	U	11 M
	12 R	A	13 P	E		E		A		M	O		T	A
	I		I	S		X		A		C			O	R
	T		N					C		14 S	15 O	N		Y
	T	16 G	U	S				H			U			
	E		P							17 N	A	T	I	18 E
	N		O								S		E	
			N		19 F				20 B	I		R	
21 P	E	G	G	Y	U			22 B	L	I	N	D		A
I					R	23 C		U		G	E			
L			24 J	A	N	E		D		G				
L					A	L		D		E				
O		25 B| U	C	K	L	E	Y		26 R| A	N	S	O	M
W					E									

Across
1. Book I title
3. Bigger feels ___ and resentful when he is with his family.
7. Preacher from Bigger's mother's church
10. Bigger, Gus, Jack and GH plan to rob ___'s Store
12. Bigger was charged with the ___ and murder of Mary.
14. Native ___
16. Gang friend of Bigger
17. ___ Son
21. Housekeeper
22. Mrs. Dalton's handicap
24. Mary's friend who was a communist
25. State prosecutor
26. Bigger plans to get $10,000 from Mr. Dalton as ___ money.

Down
1. Book III title
2. The evidence that leads to Bigger's downfall
4. White folks live right down here in my ___.
5. Mr. ___ owns Thomas home; Mary's father
6. Investigator
8. Bigger's lawyer
9. Owns poolroom
11. Rich white girl who is murdered
13. Mr. Dalton sent these tables to the boys' club.
15. Half the time I feel like I'm on the ___ of the world peeping in.
18. Bigger's sister
19. Where Bigger put Mary's body
20. He murders twice.
21. Murder weapon in Mary's murder
22. Bigger's brother
23. Jail room

Native Son Crossword 2

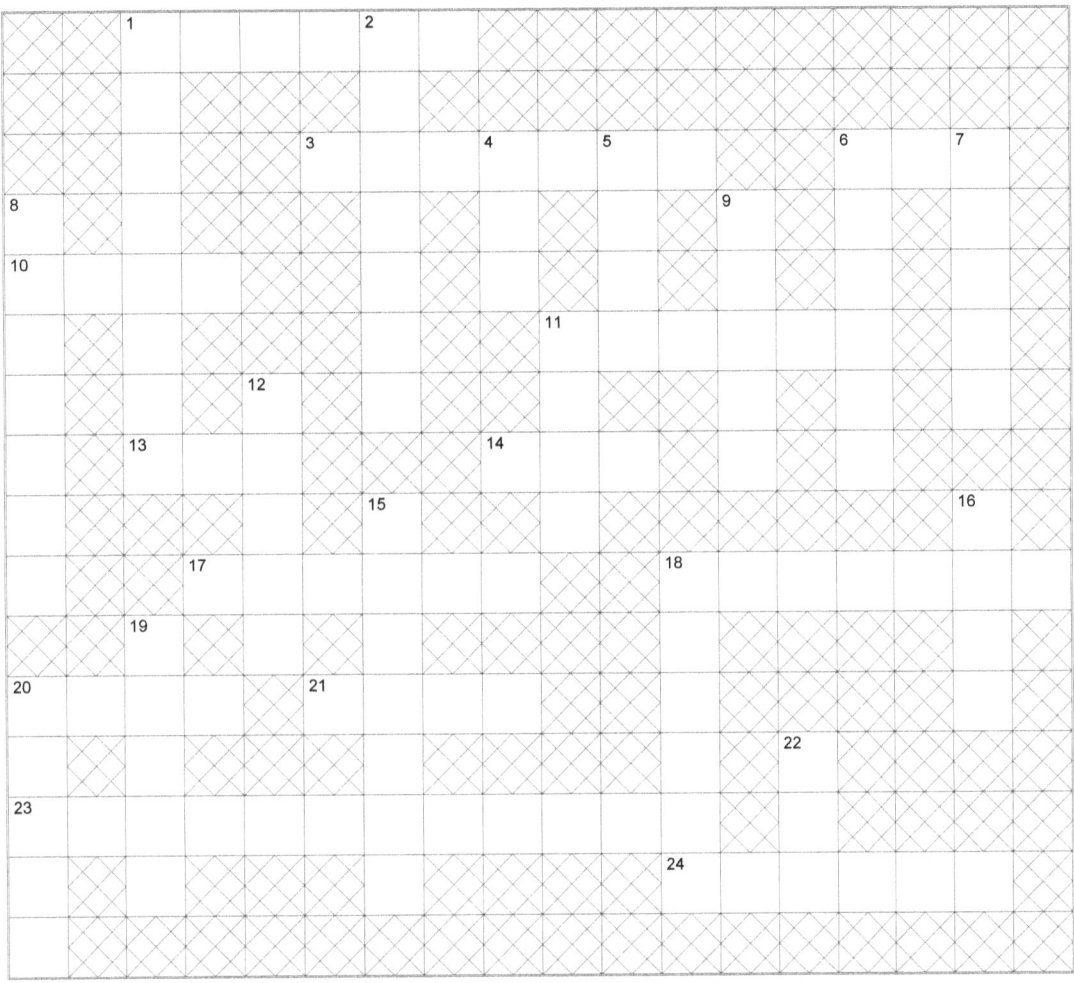

Across
1. Murder weapon in Mary's murder
3. White folks live right down here in my ___.
6. Owns poolroom
10. Bigger was charged with the ___ and murder of Mary.
11. Book II title
13. Gang friend of Bigger
14. Mary's friend who was a communist
17. Bigger's girlfriend
18. State prosecutor
20. Bigger, Gus, Jack and GH plan to rob ___'s Store
21. Book III title
23. These were the rhythms of his life: ___ and violence.
24. Bigger plans to get $10,000 from Mr. Dalton as ___ money.

Down
1. Mr. Dalton sent these tables to the boys' club.
2. Half the time I feel like I'm on the ___ of the world peeping in.
4. Bigger's lawyer
5. Jail room
6. Mr. ___ owns Thomas home; Mary's father
7. Trial room
8. Investigator
9. Housekeeper
11. Book I title
12. The evidence that leads to Bigger's downfall
15. Bigger feels ___ and resentful when he is with his family.
16. Bigger's sister
18. He murders twice.
19. Bigger's brother
20. Mrs. Dalton's handicap
22. Native ___

Native Son Crossword 2 Answer Key

		1 P	I	L	L	2 O	W						
		I				U							
		N		3 S	T	O	4 M	A	5 C	H		6 D	7 C
8 B		G		S		A		E			9 P	A	O
10 R	A	P	E	I		X		L			E	L	U
I		O		D			11 F	L	I	G	H	T	R
T		N	12 A	E			E				G	O	T
T	13 G	U	S			14 J	A	N			Y	N	
E			H	15 A			R						16 V
N	17 B	E	S	S	I	E		18 B	U	C	K	L	E Y
	19 B		S	H				I					R
20 B	L	U	M	21 F	A	T	E	G					A
L	D			M				G	22 S				
23 I	N	D	I	F	F	E	R	E	N	C	E	O	
N	Y			D				24 R	A	N	S	O	M
D													

Across
1. Murder weapon in Mary's murder
3. White folks live right down here in my ___.
6. Owns poolroom
10. Bigger was charged with the ___ and murder of Mary.
11. Book II title
13. Gang friend of Bigger
14. Mary's friend who was a communist
17. Bigger's girlfriend
18. State prosecutor
20. Bigger, Gus, Jack and GH plan to rob ___'s Store
21. Book III title
23. These were the rhythms of his life: ___ and violence.
24. Bigger plans to get $10,000 from Mr. Dalton as ___ money.

Down
1. Mr. Dalton sent these tables to the boys' club.
2. Half the time I feel like I'm on the ___ of the world peeping in.
4. Bigger's lawyer
5. Jail room
6. Mr. ___ owns Thomas home; Mary's father
7. Trial room
8. Investigator
9. Housekeeper
11. Book I title
12. The evidence that leads to Bigger's downfall
15. Bigger feels ___ and resentful when he is with his family.
16. Bigger's sister
18. He murders twice.
19. Bigger's brother
20. Mrs. Dalton's handicap
22. Native ___

Native Son Crossword 3

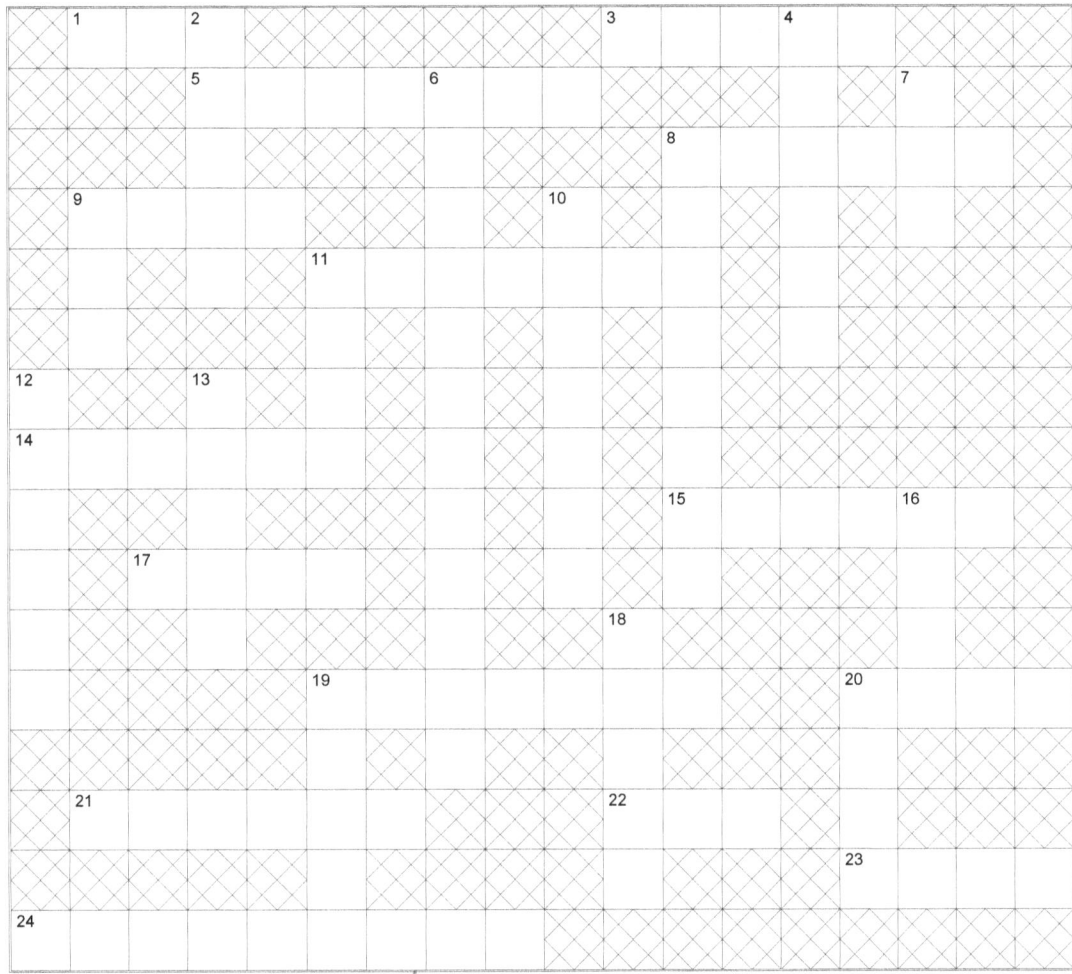

Across
1. Owns poolroom
3. Bigger's brother
5. Half the time I feel like I'm on the ___ of the world peeping in.
8. Murder weapon in Mary's murder
9. Rich white girl who is murdered
11. Investigator
14. Bigger plans to get $10,000 from Mr. Dalton as ___ money.
15. ___ Son
17. Jail room
19. State prosecutor
20. Book III title
21. Bigger's girlfriend
22. Gang friend of Bigger
23. Bigger was charged with the ___ and murder of Mary.
24. Preconceived idea

Down
2. Trial room
4. Mr. ___ owns Thomas home; Mary's father
6. These were the rhythms of his life: ___ and violence.
7. Native ___
8. Mr. Dalton sent these tables to the boys' club.
9. Bigger's lawyer
10. White folks live right down here in my ___.
11. Bigger, Gus, Jack and GH plan to rob ___'s Store
12. Author Richard
13. The evidence that leads to Bigger's downfall
16. Bigger's sister
18. Housekeeper
19. Mrs. Dalton's handicap
20. Book I title

Native Son Crossword 3 Answer Key

Across
1. Owns poolroom
3. Bigger's brother
5. Half the time I feel like I'm on the ___ of the world peeping in.
8. Murder weapon in Mary's murder
9. Rich white girl who is murdered
11. Investigator
14. Bigger plans to get $10,000 from Mr. Dalton as ___ money.
15. ___ Son
17. Jail room
19. State prosecutor
20. Book III title
21. Bigger's girlfriend
22. Gang friend of Bigger
23. Bigger was charged with the ___ and murder of Mary.
24. Preconceived idea

Down
2. Trial room
4. Mr. ___ owns Thomas home; Mary's father
6. These were the rhythms of his life: ___ and violence.
7. Native ___
8. Mr. Dalton sent these tables to the boys' club.
9. Bigger's lawyer
10. White folks live right down here in my ___.
11. Bigger, Gus, Jack and GH plan to rob ___'s Store
12. Author Richard
13. The evidence that leads to Bigger's downfall
16. Bigger's sister
18. Housekeeper
19. Mrs. Dalton's handicap
20. Book I title

Native Son Crossword 4

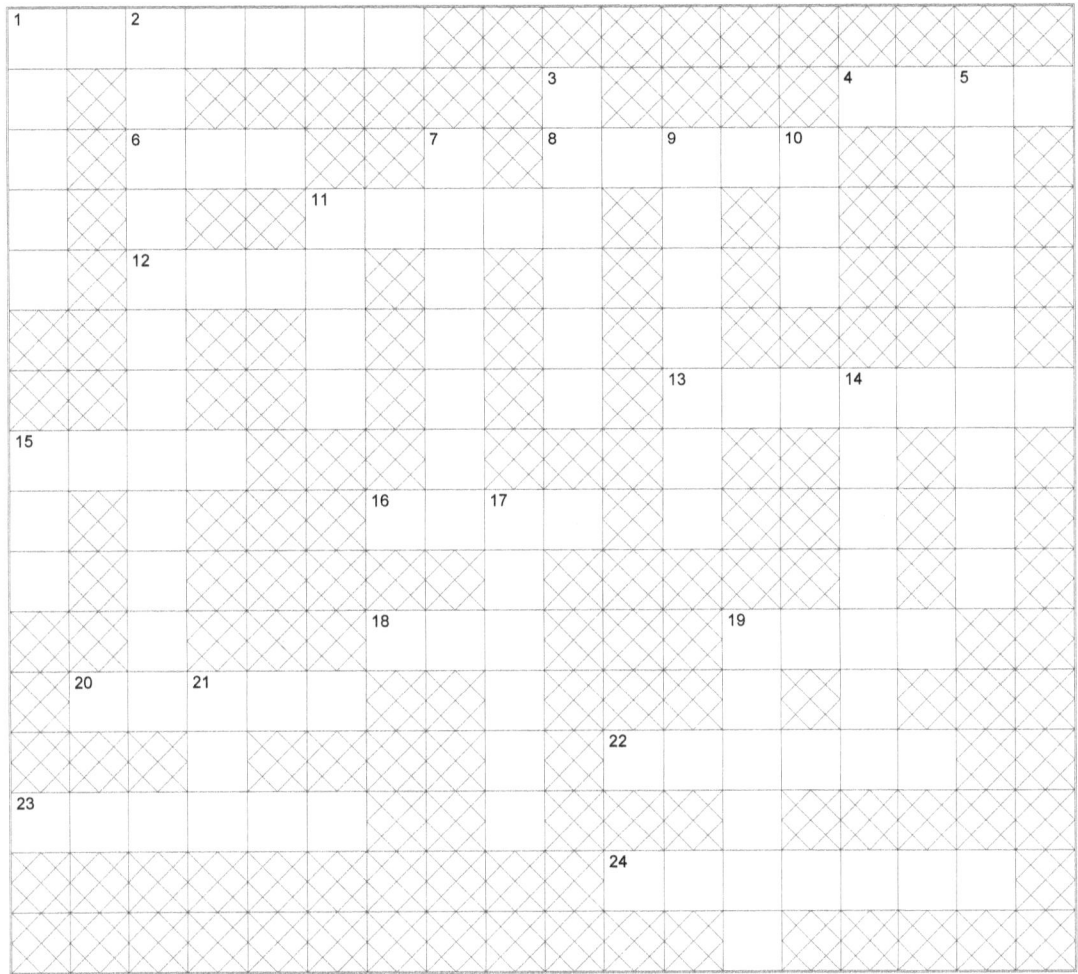

Across
1. Investigator
4. Bigger was charged with the ___ and murder of Mary.
6. Owns poolroom
8. The evidence that leads to Bigger's downfall
11. Trial room
12. Book III title
13. Half the time I feel like I'm on the ___ of the world peeping in.
15. Rich white girl who is murdered
16. Bigger's sister
18. Mary's friend who was a communist
19. Book I title
20. Housekeeper
22. Author Richard
23. Bigger's girlfriend
24. Bigger feels ___ and resentful when he is with his family.

Down
1. Bigger's brother
2. These were the rhythms of his life: ___ and violence.
3. ___ Son
5. Preconceived idea
7. Where Bigger put Mary's body
9. Preacher from Bigger's mother's church
10. Native ___
11. Jail room
14. White folks live right down here in my ___.
15. Bigger's lawyer
17. Bigger plans to get $10,000 from Mr. Dalton as ___ money.
19. Book II title
21. Gang friend of Bigger

Native Son Crossword 4 Answer Key

	1 B	R	2 I	T	T	E	N							
	U		N						3 N				4 R	A	5 P	E
	D		6 D	O	C		7 F		8 A	S	9 H	E	10 S		R	
	D		I		11 C	O	U	R	T		A		O		E	
	Y		12 F	A	T	E		R		I		M		N		J	
			F			L		N		V		M				U	
			E			L		A		E		13 O	U	14 T	S	I	D	E
	15 M	A	R	Y				C				N		T		I	
	A		E			16 V	E	17 R	A		D		O		C	
	X		N					A				M		E	
			C			18 J	A	N			19 F	E	A	R	
		20 P	E	21 G	G	Y		S			L		C	
				U				O		22 W	R	I	G	H	T
		23 B	E	S	S	I	E		M			G	
										24 A	S	H	A	M	E	D
										T			

Across
1. Investigator
4. Bigger was charged with the ___ and murder of Mary.
6. Owns poolroom
8. The evidence that leads to Bigger's downfall
11. Trial room
12. Book III title
13. Half the time I feel like I'm on the ___ of the world peeping in.
15. Rich white girl who is murdered
16. Bigger's sister
18. Mary's friend who was a communist
19. Book I title
20. Housekeeper
22. Author Richard
23. Bigger's girlfriend
24. Bigger feels ___ and resentful when he is with his family.

Down
1. Bigger's brother
2. These were the rhythms of his life: ___ and violence.
3. ___ Son
5. Preconceived idea
7. Where Bigger put Mary's body
9. Preacher from Bigger's mother's church
10. Native ___
11. Jail room
14. White folks live right down here in my ___.
15. Bigger's lawyer
17. Bigger plans to get $10,000 from Mr. Dalton as ___ money.
19. Book II title
21. Gang friend of Bigger

Native Son

BESSIE	PEGGY	FLIGHT	RAPE	INDIFFERENCE
FEAR	PREJUDICE	OUTSIDE	HAMMOND	BLUM
STOMACH	PINGPONG	FREE SPACE	BLIND	MARY
COURT	JAN	MAX	PILLOW	GUS
SON	BRITTEN	ASHES	DALTON	NATIVE

Native Son

FURNACE	BIGGER	DOC	BUDDY	FATE
WRIGHT	CELL	VERA	ASHAMED	BUCKLEY
NATIVE	DALTON	FREE SPACE	BRITTEN	SON
GUS	PILLOW	MAX	JAN	COURT
MARY	BLIND	RANSOM	PINGPONG	STOMACH

Native Son

WRIGHT	BLUM	INDIFFERENCE	OUTSIDE	JAN
STOMACH	VERA	BUDDY	COURT	RANSOM
ASHES	BRITTEN	FREE SPACE	MAX	PREJUDICE
PEGGY	PILLOW	FLIGHT	ASHAMED	BUCKLEY
FURNACE	SON	BIGGER	PINGPONG	CELL

Native Son

NATIVE	DALTON	BESSIE	FEAR	BLIND
MARY	DOC	FATE	HAMMOND	GUS
CELL	PINGPONG	FREE SPACE	SON	FURNACE
BUCKLEY	ASHAMED	FLIGHT	PILLOW	PEGGY
PREJUDICE	MAX	RAPE	BRITTEN	ASHES

Native Son

BUCKLEY	FATE	OUTSIDE	STOMACH	MARY
PINGPONG	ASHAMED	NATIVE	FEAR	FLIGHT
BESSIE	PILLOW	FREE SPACE	PEGGY	CELL
INDIFFERENCE	SON	RAPE	VERA	MAX
HAMMOND	DALTON	COURT	DOC	FURNACE

Native Son

BRITTEN	JAN	BIGGER	RANSOM	BLUM
PREJUDICE	BLIND	GUS	ASHES	BUDDY
FURNACE	DOC	FREE SPACE	DALTON	HAMMOND
MAX	VERA	RAPE	SON	INDIFFERENCE
CELL	PEGGY	WRIGHT	PILLOW	BESSIE

Native Son

FEAR	FURNACE	BRITTEN	BLIND	NATIVE
OUTSIDE	PREJUDICE	BLUM	MAX	HAMMOND
PEGGY	FATE	FREE SPACE	ASHES	ASHAMED
FLIGHT	SON	PINGPONG	BUDDY	GUS
DOC	CELL	INDIFFERENCE	BUCKLEY	RAPE

Native Son

MARY	BESSIE	STOMACH	COURT	BIGGER
DALTON	RANSOM	PILLOW	VERA	JAN
RAPE	BUCKLEY	FREE SPACE	CELL	DOC
GUS	BUDDY	PINGPONG	SON	FLIGHT
ASHAMED	ASHES	WRIGHT	FATE	PEGGY

Native Son

PINGPONG	BLUM	BLIND	WRIGHT	MARY
PILLOW	BUDDY	HAMMOND	FURNACE	ASHAMED
FEAR	PREJUDICE	FREE SPACE	BESSIE	BUCKLEY
BIGGER	RAPE	NATIVE	OUTSIDE	VERA
INDIFFERENCE	ASHES	RANSOM	SON	COURT

Native Son

CELL	STOMACH	JAN	DALTON	FATE
GUS	BRITTEN	DOC	FLIGHT	MAX
COURT	SON	FREE SPACE	ASHES	INDIFFERENCE
VERA	OUTSIDE	NATIVE	RAPE	BIGGER
BUCKLEY	BESSIE	PEGGY	PREJUDICE	FEAR

Native Son

JAN	DOC	BUCKLEY	PINGPONG	BESSIE
BUDDY	RANSOM	FEAR	FLIGHT	WRIGHT
CELL	BIGGER	FREE SPACE	PEGGY	FATE
BLUM	DALTON	INDIFFERENCE	HAMMOND	ASHES
GUS	MAX	NATIVE	RAPE	MARY

Native Son

COURT	PILLOW	SON	FURNACE	BRITTEN
OUTSIDE	PREJUDICE	BLIND	STOMACH	ASHAMED
MARY	RAPE	FREE SPACE	MAX	GUS
ASHES	HAMMOND	INDIFFERENCE	DALTON	BLUM
FATE	PEGGY	VERA	BIGGER	CELL

Native Son

COURT	ASHES	PINGPONG	SON	BLIND
PREJUDICE	PEGGY	BUDDY	DALTON	MARY
BUCKLEY	FEAR	FREE SPACE	PILLOW	ASHAMED
HAMMOND	FURNACE	BESSIE	INDIFFERENCE	JAN
OUTSIDE	BLUM	RANSOM	FATE	BIGGER

Native Son

RAPE	BRITTEN	CELL	FLIGHT	WRIGHT
DOC	VERA	GUS	STOMACH	MAX
BIGGER	FATE	FREE SPACE	BLUM	OUTSIDE
JAN	INDIFFERENCE	BESSIE	FURNACE	HAMMOND
ASHAMED	PILLOW	NATIVE	FEAR	BUCKLEY

Native Son

VERA	JAN	MARY	NATIVE	ASHES
FURNACE	CELL	BRITTEN	BLIND	RANSOM
FLIGHT	DALTON	FREE SPACE	WRIGHT	FEAR
BESSIE	PINGPONG	DOC	SON	BUCKLEY
HAMMOND	INDIFFERENCE	FATE	MAX	PREJUDICE

Native Son

PEGGY	BUDDY	ASHAMED	PILLOW	COURT
OUTSIDE	BLUM	STOMACH	BIGGER	GUS
PREJUDICE	MAX	FREE SPACE	INDIFFERENCE	HAMMOND
BUCKLEY	SON	DOC	PINGPONG	BESSIE
FEAR	WRIGHT	RAPE	DALTON	FLIGHT

Native Son

GUS	BLUM	RANSOM	NATIVE	FLIGHT
FATE	SON	COURT	FEAR	DOC
WRIGHT	MAX	FREE SPACE	BLIND	INDIFFERENCE
HAMMOND	PILLOW	BUCKLEY	BUDDY	MARY
BESSIE	OUTSIDE	ASHES	ASHAMED	PEGGY

Native Son

FURNACE	DALTON	PREJUDICE	STOMACH	BRITTEN
CELL	BIGGER	PINGPONG	RAPE	JAN
PEGGY	ASHAMED	FREE SPACE	OUTSIDE	BESSIE
MARY	BUDDY	BUCKLEY	PILLOW	HAMMOND
INDIFFERENCE	BLIND	VERA	MAX	WRIGHT

Native Son

PILLOW	DOC	WRIGHT	BUDDY	BRITTEN
SON	INDIFFERENCE	FLIGHT	FEAR	BESSIE
COURT	PREJUDICE	FREE SPACE	RAPE	BIGGER
BLUM	ASHAMED	DALTON	RANSOM	MAX
HAMMOND	PINGPONG	FATE	STOMACH	PEGGY

Native Son

NATIVE	CELL	JAN	OUTSIDE	ASHES
FURNACE	VERA	BUCKLEY	MARY	BLIND
PEGGY	STOMACH	FREE SPACE	PINGPONG	HAMMOND
MAX	RANSOM	DALTON	ASHAMED	BLUM
BIGGER	RAPE	GUS	PREJUDICE	COURT

Native Son

VERA	DALTON	COURT	RAPE	STOMACH
JAN	RANSOM	BESSIE	GUS	BLIND
PILLOW	BRITTEN	FREE SPACE	OUTSIDE	BUCKLEY
WRIGHT	PEGGY	BLUM	BIGGER	FURNACE
ASHES	HAMMOND	SON	PINGPONG	FLIGHT

Native Son

BUDDY	ASHAMED	FEAR	DOC	CELL
PREJUDICE	FATE	NATIVE	MAX	INDIFFERENCE
FLIGHT	PINGPONG	FREE SPACE	HAMMOND	ASHES
FURNACE	BIGGER	BLUM	PEGGY	WRIGHT
BUCKLEY	OUTSIDE	MARY	BRITTEN	PILLOW

Native Son

HAMMOND	FURNACE	BUDDY	COURT	BRITTEN
PEGGY	MARY	FLIGHT	ASHAMED	BUCKLEY
DOC	JAN	FREE SPACE	WRIGHT	PREJUDICE
STOMACH	BLUM	PILLOW	BIGGER	SON
FEAR	RANSOM	INDIFFERENCE	PINGPONG	DALTON

Native Son

BLIND	MAX	OUTSIDE	RAPE	CELL
ASHES	BESSIE	NATIVE	GUS	VERA
DALTON	PINGPONG	FREE SPACE	RANSOM	FEAR
SON	BIGGER	PILLOW	BLUM	STOMACH
PREJUDICE	WRIGHT	FATE	JAN	DOC

Native Son

PREJUDICE	BESSIE	JAN	SON	RAPE
MARY	NATIVE	BLIND	HAMMOND	PEGGY
GUS	DALTON	FREE SPACE	BUCKLEY	WRIGHT
BUDDY	STOMACH	FEAR	ASHES	VERA
BLUM	DOC	BIGGER	CELL	FURNACE

Native Son

PILLOW	ASHAMED	FLIGHT	INDIFFERENCE	PINGPONG
BRITTEN	RANSOM	MAX	OUTSIDE	FATE
FURNACE	CELL	FREE SPACE	DOC	BLUM
VERA	ASHES	FEAR	STOMACH	BUDDY
WRIGHT	BUCKLEY	COURT	DALTON	GUS

Native Son

GUS	SON	COURT	HAMMOND	BRITTEN
DALTON	BIGGER	FEAR	DOC	BUCKLEY
FURNACE	MAX	FREE SPACE	INDIFFERENCE	PILLOW
FLIGHT	PEGGY	BESSIE	JAN	CELL
RAPE	MARY	WRIGHT	PREJUDICE	STOMACH

Native Son

BLUM	FATE	RANSOM	OUTSIDE	BLIND
PINGPONG	VERA	BUDDY	NATIVE	ASHES
STOMACH	PREJUDICE	FREE SPACE	MARY	RAPE
CELL	JAN	BESSIE	PEGGY	FLIGHT
PILLOW	INDIFFERENCE	ASHAMED	MAX	FURNACE

Native Son

BLUM	JAN	BUDDY	ASHAMED	SON
BIGGER	INDIFFERENCE	NATIVE	BLIND	HAMMOND
CELL	BUCKLEY	FREE SPACE	FATE	FLIGHT
FURNACE	BESSIE	WRIGHT	VERA	DALTON
GUS	PINGPONG	MAX	PEGGY	DOC

Native Son

FEAR	PILLOW	COURT	MARY	OUTSIDE
RAPE	PREJUDICE	BRITTEN	ASHES	STOMACH
DOC	PEGGY	FREE SPACE	PINGPONG	GUS
DALTON	VERA	WRIGHT	BESSIE	FURNACE
FLIGHT	FATE	RANSOM	BUCKLEY	CELL

Native Son

VERA	DOC	FLIGHT	ASHES	MAX
INDIFFERENCE	PREJUDICE	OUTSIDE	CELL	STOMACH
BLUM	ASHAMED	FREE SPACE	BIGGER	SON
NATIVE	BUDDY	COURT	FATE	BLIND
JAN	WRIGHT	DALTON	FURNACE	FEAR

Native Son

BRITTEN	RANSOM	PEGGY	MARY	PILLOW
BUCKLEY	HAMMOND	GUS	RAPE	BESSIE
FEAR	FURNACE	FREE SPACE	WRIGHT	JAN
BLIND	FATE	COURT	BUDDY	NATIVE
SON	BIGGER	PINGPONG	ASHAMED	BLUM

Native Son Vocabulary Word List

No.	Word	Clue/Definition
1.	ABSTRACTEDLY	In a manner apart from the situation
2.	ACCORD	Agreement
3.	ALIBI	An excuse; a way to prove one could not have committed a crime
4.	ANARCHIST	One who is against all forms of government
5.	APPREHENSIVELY	Anxiously; fearfully
6.	ARDENTLY	Enthusiastically; fervently
7.	ARRAIGNMENT	Court proceeding in which accused persons answer the charges brought against them
8.	ASPIRATION	Ambition
9.	ATONE	Make up for; make amends for
10.	AUGMENTED	Added to; supplemented
11.	AWE	Mixed emotion of reverence, respect, and dread
12.	BELLIGERENTLY	Hostilely
13.	BENEVOLENT	Good
14.	CONDEMNED	Found guilty or unfit
15.	CONJECTURED	Thought; came to a conclusion based on present evidence
16.	CONSENTED	Agreed
17.	CONTAGION	Easily transmitted disease
18.	CONTRITE	Sorry
19.	DORMANT	Asleep; inactive
20.	DUPED	Deceived; made to look foolish
21.	EBBED	Flowed away from
22.	ELATION	Feeling of extreme happiness or pleasure
23.	ELUDED	Escaped from one's understanding
24.	ENDURE	Carry on through hardships
25.	EXHORTED	Urged through arguments or appeals
26.	FLACCID	Lacking firmness or muscle tone
27.	FOREBODING	Predicting something bad for the future
28.	FUTILE	Useless
29.	GRATIFY	Satisfy; indulge
30.	HYSTERICAL	Having uncontrolled emotions
31.	IMPALPABLE	Can't be grasped by touch or in the mind
32.	IMPELLED	Motivated; had the feeling of needing to do something
33.	IMPERIOUSLY	Overbearingly; pressingly; urgently
34.	IMPLICATE	Connect incriminatingly
35.	IMPULSE	Inclination; motivating force
36.	IMPUTED	Attributed; credited
37.	INARTICULATE	Wordless; speechless
38.	INDELIBLE	Permanent
39.	INEXTRICABLY	Not being able to escape from
40.	IRKED	Irritated; bothered
41.	IRREVOCABLE	Can't be taken or sent back
42.	LABYRINTH	Maze
43.	LATENT	Dormant; present but not active
44.	LATITUDE	Leeway; freedom within regulations
45.	LINGERING	Remaining, as though reluctant to leave
46.	LULLED	Calmed
47.	MITIGATING	Making more moderate
48.	MORASS	Something that hinders, engulfs, or overwhelms
49.	PEEVED	Vexed; angry
50.	PREMEDITATION	Planning beforehand

Native Son Vocabulary Word List Continued

No.	Word	Clue/Definition
51.	QUEER	Strange
52.	RENDERED	Made; caused to be
53.	REPROACH	Disapproval
54.	SANCTION	Approve
55.	STAVE	Put off; postpone
56.	SUBSIDED	Quieted; settled
57.	SUCCUMB	Give in; come under the influence of
58.	SULLEN	Sulky
59.	SURLY	Bad-humored; gruff
60.	TAUT	Tight; tense
61.	UNABATING	Not subsiding; not becoming less
62.	UNETHICAL	Wrong; not within accepted guidelines
63.	VENUE	Location where a trial is held
64.	VIGILANTES	People who take the law into their own hands
65.	VOWED	Promised
66.	YEARNING	Longing

Native Son Vocabulary Fill In The Blanks 1

_____

1. An excuse; a way to prove one could not have committed a crime
2. Make up for; make amends for
3. Agreed
4. Carry on through hardships
5. Overbearingly; pressingly; urgently
6. Connect incriminatingly
7. Tight; tense
8. Leeway; freedom within regulations
9. Flowed away from
10. Longing
11. Not being able to escape from
12. Feeling of extreme happiness or pleasure
13. Made; caused to be
14. Remaining, as though reluctant to leave
15. Urged through arguments or appeals
16. Sulky
17. Making more moderate
18. Anxiously; fearfully
19. Deceived; made to look foolish
20. Good

Native Son Vocabulary Fill In The Blanks 1 Answer Key

ALIBI	1. An excuse; a way to prove one could not have committed a crime
ATONE	2. Make up for; make amends for
CONSENTED	3. Agreed
ENDURE	4. Carry on through hardships
IMPERIOUSLY	5. Overbearingly; pressingly; urgently
IMPLICATE	6. Connect incriminatingly
TAUT	7. Tight; tense
LATITUDE	8. Leeway; freedom within regulations
EBBED	9. Flowed away from
YEARNING	10. Longing
INEXTRICABLY	11. Not being able to escape from
ELATION	12. Feeling of extreme happiness or pleasure
RENDERED	13. Made; caused to be
LINGERING	14. Remaining, as though reluctant to leave
EXHORTED	15. Urged through arguments or appeals
SULLEN	16. Sulky
MITIGATING	17. Making more moderate
APPREHENSIVELY	18. Anxiously; fearfully
DUPED	19. Deceived; made to look foolish
BENEVOLENT	20. Good

Native Son Vocabulary Fill In The Blanks 2

_____ 1. People who take the law into their own hands

_____ 2. Leeway; freedom within regulations

_____ 3. Not subsiding; not becoming less

_____ 4. Carry on through hardships

_____ 5. Found guilty or unfit

_____ 6. Inclination; motivating force

_____ 7. Can't be grasped by touch or in the mind

_____ 8. Feeling of extreme happiness or pleasure

_____ 9. Permanent

_____ 10. Predicting something bad for the future

_____ 11. Asleep; inactive

_____ 12. Deceived; made to look foolish

_____ 13. Motivated; had the feeling of needing to do something

_____ 14. Court proceeding in which accused persons answer the charges brought against them

_____ 15. Maze

_____ 16. In a manner apart from the situation

_____ 17. Dormant; present but not active

_____ 18. Bad-humored; gruff

_____ 19. Put off; postpone

_____ 20. Having uncontrolled emotions

Native Son Vocabulary Fill In The Blanks 2 Answer Key

VIGILANTES	1. People who take the law into their own hands
LATITUDE	2. Leeway; freedom within regulations
UNABATING	3. Not subsiding; not becoming less
ENDURE	4. Carry on through hardships
CONDEMNED	5. Found guilty or unfit
IMPULSE	6. Inclination; motivating force
IMPALPABLE	7. Can't be grasped by touch or in the mind
ELATION	8. Feeling of extreme happiness or pleasure
INDELIBLE	9. Permanent
FOREBODING	10. Predicting something bad for the future
DORMANT	11. Asleep; inactive
DUPED	12. Deceived; made to look foolish
IMPELLED	13. Motivated; had the feeling of needing to do something
ARRAIGNMENT	14. Court proceeding in which accused persons answer the charges brought against them
LABYRINTH	15. Maze
ABSTRACTEDLY	16. In a manner apart from the situation
LATENT	17. Dormant; present but not active
SURLY	18. Bad-humored; gruff
STAVE	19. Put off; postpone
HYSTERICAL	20. Having uncontrolled emotions

Native Son Vocabulary Fill In The Blanks 3

1. Flowed away from
2. Planning beforehand
3. Remaining, as though reluctant to leave
4. Wordless; speechless
5. Urged through arguments or appeals
6. An excuse; a way to prove one could not have committed a crime
7. Asleep; inactive
8. Put off; postpone
9. Longing
10. Good
11. Mixed emotion of reverence, respect, and dread
12. Sulky
13. Made; caused to be
14. Connect incriminatingly
15. Satisfy; indulge
16. Strange
17. Can't be grasped by touch or in the mind
18. Carry on through hardships
19. Approve
20. Overbearingly; pressingly; urgently

Native Son Vocabulary Fill In The Blanks 3 Answer Key

EBBED	1. Flowed away from
PREMEDITATION	2. Planning beforehand
LINGERING	3. Remaining, as though reluctant to leave
INARTICULATE	4. Wordless; speechless
EXHORTED	5. Urged through arguments or appeals
ALIBI	6. An excuse; a way to prove one could not have committed a crime
DORMANT	7. Asleep; inactive
STAVE	8. Put off; postpone
YEARNING	9. Longing
BENEVOLENT	10. Good
AWE	11. Mixed emotion of reverence, respect, and dread
SULLEN	12. Sulky
RENDERED	13. Made; caused to be
IMPLICATE	14. Connect incriminatingly
GRATIFY	15. Satisfy; indulge
QUEER	16. Strange
IMPALPABLE	17. Can't be grasped by touch or in the mind
ENDURE	18. Carry on through hardships
SANCTION	19. Approve
IMPERIOUSLY	20. Overbearingly; pressingly; urgently

Native Son Vocabulary Fill In The Blanks 4

1. Quieted; settled
2. Attributed; credited
3. Hostilely
4. Good
5. Court proceeding in which accused persons answer the charges brought against them
6. Agreement
7. Bad-humored; gruff
8. Deceived; made to look foolish
9. Predicting something bad for the future
10. Flowed away from
11. Sulky
12. Irritated; bothered
13. Added to; supplemented
14. Leeway; freedom within regulations
15. Satisfy; indulge
16. Make up for; make amends for
17. Not subsiding; not becoming less
18. Strange
19. Can't be taken or sent back
20. Location where a trial is held

Native Son Vocabulary Fill In The Blanks 4 Answer Key

SUBSIDED	1. Quieted; settled
IMPUTED	2. Attributed; credited
BELLIGERENTLY	3. Hostilely
BENEVOLENT	4. Good
ARRAIGNMENT	5. Court proceeding in which accused persons answer the charges brought against them
ACCORD	6. Agreement
SURLY	7. Bad-humored; gruff
DUPED	8. Deceived; made to look foolish
FOREBODING	9. Predicting something bad for the future
EBBED	10. Flowed away from
SULLEN	11. Sulky
IRKED	12. Irritated; bothered
AUGMENTED	13. Added to; supplemented
LATITUDE	14. Leeway; freedom within regulations
GRATIFY	15. Satisfy; indulge
ATONE	16. Make up for; make amends for
UNABATING	17. Not subsiding; not becoming less
QUEER	18. Strange
IRREVOCABLE	19. Can't be taken or sent back
VENUE	20. Location where a trial is held

Native Son Vocabulary Matching 1

___ 1. ABSTRACTEDLY
___ 2. BENEVOLENT
___ 3. LINGERING
___ 4. ALIBI
___ 5. LATITUDE
___ 6. CONJECTURED
___ 7. TAUT
___ 8. AUGMENTED
___ 9. INDELIBLE
___ 10. ACCORD
___ 11. IMPLICATE
___ 12. ASPIRATION
___ 13. ELUDED
___ 14. INEXTRICABLY
___ 15. UNABATING
___ 16. STAVE
___ 17. ATONE
___ 18. DUPED
___ 19. IMPELLED
___ 20. FUTILE
___ 21. PREMEDITATION
___ 22. VIGILANTES
___ 23. EBBED
___ 24. VENUE
___ 25. AWE

A. Ambition
B. Not subsiding; not becoming less
C. Agreement
D. People who take the law into their own hands
E. Escaped from one's understanding
F. Thought; came to a conclusion based on present evidence
G. Motivated; had the feeling of needing to do something
H. Useless
I. Make up for; make amends for
J. Leeway; freedom within regulations
K. Mixed emotion of reverence, respect, and dread
L. An excuse; a way to prove one could not have committed a crime
M. In a manner apart from the situation
N. Connect incriminatingly
O. Added to; supplemented
P. Planning beforehand
Q. Flowed away from
R. Location where a trial is held
S. Permanent
T. Deceived; made to look foolish
U. Good
V. Tight; tense
W. Remaining, as though reluctant to leave
X. Put off; postpone
Y. Not being able to escape from

Native Son Vocabulary Matching 1 Answer Key

M - 1.	ABSTRACTEDLY	A.	Ambition
U - 2.	BENEVOLENT	B.	Not subsiding; not becoming less
W - 3.	LINGERING	C.	Agreement
L - 4.	ALIBI	D.	People who take the law into their own hands
J - 5.	LATITUDE	E.	Escaped from one's understanding
F - 6.	CONJECTURED	F.	Thought; came to a conclusion based on present evidence
V - 7.	TAUT	G.	Motivated; had the feeling of needing to do something
O - 8.	AUGMENTED	H.	Useless
S - 9.	INDELIBLE	I.	Make up for; make amends for
C -10.	ACCORD	J.	Leeway; freedom within regulations
N -11.	IMPLICATE	K.	Mixed emotion of reverence, respect, and dread
A -12.	ASPIRATION	L.	An excuse; a way to prove one could not have committed a crime
E -13.	ELUDED	M.	In a manner apart from the situation
Y -14.	INEXTRICABLY	N.	Connect incriminatingly
B -15.	UNABATING	O.	Added to; supplemented
X -16.	STAVE	P.	Planning beforehand
I - 17.	ATONE	Q.	Flowed away from
T -18.	DUPED	R.	Location where a trial is held
G -19.	IMPELLED	S.	Permanent
H -20.	FUTILE	T.	Deceived; made to look foolish
P -21.	PREMEDITATION	U.	Good
D -22.	VIGILANTES	V.	Tight; tense
Q -23.	EBBED	W.	Remaining, as though reluctant to leave
R -24.	VENUE	X.	Put off; postpone
K -25.	AWE	Y.	Not being able to escape from

Native Son Vocabulary Matching 2

___ 1. REPROACH
___ 2. VIGILANTES
___ 3. LATITUDE
___ 4. ARRAIGNMENT
___ 5. LINGERING
___ 6. RENDERED
___ 7. IMPULSE
___ 8. IRKED
___ 9. UNETHICAL
___10. DORMANT
___11. INDELIBLE
___12. PREMEDITATION
___13. INEXTRICABLY
___14. AUGMENTED
___15. CONDEMNED
___16. HYSTERICAL
___17. EXHORTED
___18. IMPALPABLE
___19. ACCORD
___20. FLACCID
___21. ELATION
___22. YEARNING
___23. ASPIRATION
___24. INARTICULATE
___25. SUBSIDED

A. Made; caused to be
B. Permanent
C. Urged through arguments or appeals
D. Wordless; speechless
E. Asleep; inactive
F. Planning beforehand
G. Court proceeding in which accused persons answer the charges brought against them
H. Wrong; not within accepted guidelines
I. Ambition
J. Feeling of extreme happiness or pleasure
K. Leeway; freedom within regulations
L. People who take the law into their own hands
M. Irritated; bothered
N. Found guilty or unfit
O. Not being able to escape from
P. Inclination; motivating force
Q. Having uncontrolled emotions
R. Remaining, as though reluctant to leave
S. Longing
T. Lacking firmness or muscle tone
U. Quieted; settled
V. Agreement
W. Disapproval
X. Can't be grasped by touch or in the mind
Y. Added to; supplemented

Native Son Vocabulary Matching 2 Answer Key

W - 1. REPROACH
L - 2. VIGILANTES
K - 3. LATITUDE
G - 4. ARRAIGNMENT
R - 5. LINGERING
A - 6. RENDERED
P - 7. IMPULSE
M - 8. IRKED
H - 9. UNETHICAL
E - 10. DORMANT
B - 11. INDELIBLE
F - 12. PREMEDITATION
O - 13. INEXTRICABLY
Y - 14. AUGMENTED
N - 15. CONDEMNED
Q - 16. HYSTERICAL
C - 17. EXHORTED
X - 18. IMPALPABLE
V - 19. ACCORD
T - 20. FLACCID
J - 21. ELATION
S - 22. YEARNING
I - 23. ASPIRATION
D - 24. INARTICULATE
U - 25. SUBSIDED

A. Made; caused to be
B. Permanent
C. Urged through arguments or appeals
D. Wordless; speechless
E. Asleep; inactive
F. Planning beforehand
G. Court proceeding in which accused persons answer the charges brought against them
H. Wrong; not within accepted guidelines
I. Ambition
J. Feeling of extreme happiness or pleasure
K. Leeway; freedom within regulations
L. People who take the law into their own hands
M. Irritated; bothered
N. Found guilty or unfit
O. Not being able to escape from
P. Inclination; motivating force
Q. Having uncontrolled emotions
R. Remaining, as though reluctant to leave
S. Longing
T. Lacking firmness or muscle tone
U. Quieted; settled
V. Agreement
W. Disapproval
X. Can't be grasped by touch or in the mind
Y. Added to; supplemented

Native Son Vocabulary Matching 3

___ 1. REPROACH   A. Not being able to escape from
___ 2. EXHORTED   B. Predicting something bad for the future
___ 3. DUPED   C. Can't be taken or sent back
___ 4. VOWED   D. Sorry
___ 5. IRREVOCABLE   E. Ambition
___ 6. GRATIFY   F. Overbearingly; pressingly; urgently
___ 7. SULLEN   G. Wordless; speechless
___ 8. INARTICULATE   H. Anxiously; fearfully
___ 9. IMPERIOUSLY   I. Added to; supplemented
___10. MORASS   J. Something that hinders, engulfs, or overwhelms
___11. FOREBODING   K. Disapproval
___12. PREMEDITATION   L. Permanent
___13. DORMANT   M. Sulky
___14. ASPIRATION   N. Asleep; inactive
___15. IMPUTED   O. Easily transmitted disease
___16. INEXTRICABLY   P. Attributed; credited
___17. ALIBI   Q. Satisfy; indulge
___18. LABYRINTH   R. An excuse; a way to prove one could not have committed a crime
___19. UNETHICAL   S. Promised
___20. CONTRITE   T. Urged through arguments or appeals
___21. APPREHENSIVELY   U. Deceived; made to look foolish
___22. AUGMENTED   V. Flowed away from
___23. EBBED   W. Maze
___24. INDELIBLE   X. Planning beforehand
___25. CONTAGION   Y. Wrong; not within accepted guidelines

Native Son Vocabulary Matching 3 Answer Key

K - 1. REPROACH	A.	Not being able to escape from
T - 2. EXHORTED	B.	Predicting something bad for the future
U - 3. DUPED	C.	Can't be taken or sent back
S - 4. VOWED	D.	Sorry
C - 5. IRREVOCABLE	E.	Ambition
Q - 6. GRATIFY	F.	Overbearingly; pressingly; urgently
M - 7. SULLEN	G.	Wordless; speechless
G - 8. INARTICULATE	H.	Anxiously; fearfully
F - 9. IMPERIOUSLY	I.	Added to; supplemented
J - 10. MORASS	J.	Something that hinders, engulfs, or overwhelms
B - 11. FOREBODING	K.	Disapproval
X - 12. PREMEDITATION	L.	Permanent
N - 13. DORMANT	M.	Sulky
E - 14. ASPIRATION	N.	Asleep; inactive
P - 15. IMPUTED	O.	Easily transmitted disease
A - 16. INEXTRICABLY	P.	Attributed; credited
R - 17. ALIBI	Q.	Satisfy; indulge
W - 18. LABYRINTH	R.	An excuse; a way to prove one could not have committed a crime
Y - 19. UNETHICAL	S.	Promised
D - 20. CONTRITE	T.	Urged through arguments or appeals
H - 21. APPREHENSIVELY	U.	Deceived; made to look foolish
I - 22. AUGMENTED	V.	Flowed away from
V - 23. EBBED	W.	Maze
L - 24. INDELIBLE	X.	Planning beforehand
O - 25. CONTAGION	Y.	Wrong; not within accepted guidelines

Native Son Vocabulary Matching 4

___ 1. UNABATING   A. Put off; postpone

___ 2. IRREVOCABLE   B. Satisfy; indulge

___ 3. REPROACH   C. Motivated; had the feeling of needing to do something

___ 4. BELLIGERENTLY   D. Deceived; made to look foolish

___ 5. IMPELLED   E. Asleep; inactive

___ 6. INEXTRICABLY   F. Quieted; settled

___ 7. HYSTERICAL   G. Hostilely

___ 8. LABYRINTH   H. Longing

___ 9. RENDERED   I. Disapproval

___ 10. FLACCID   J. Leeway; freedom within regulations

___ 11. IMPALPABLE   K. Ambition

___ 12. ELUDED   L. Not subsiding; not becoming less

___ 13. VOWED   M. Escaped from one's understanding

___ 14. SUBSIDED   N. Maze

___ 15. DORMANT   O. Found guilty or unfit

___ 16. DUPED   P. Lacking firmness or muscle tone

___ 17. LATITUDE   Q. Overbearingly; pressingly; urgently

___ 18. CONDEMNED   R. Having uncontrolled emotions

___ 19. ASPIRATION   S. Good

___ 20. GRATIFY   T. Made; caused to be

___ 21. YEARNING   U. Can't be grasped by touch or in the mind

___ 22. STAVE   V. Promised

___ 23. IMPERIOUSLY   W. Can't be taken or sent back

___ 24. BENEVOLENT   X. Not being able to escape from

___ 25. ALIBI   Y. An excuse; a way to prove one could not have committed a crime

Native Son Vocabulary Matching 4 Answer Key

L - 1. UNABATING	A.	Put off; postpone
W - 2. IRREVOCABLE	B.	Satisfy; indulge
I - 3. REPROACH	C.	Motivated; had the feeling of needing to do something
G - 4. BELLIGERENTLY	D.	Deceived; made to look foolish
C - 5. IMPELLED	E.	Asleep; inactive
X - 6. INEXTRICABLY	F.	Quieted; settled
R - 7. HYSTERICAL	G.	Hostilely
N - 8. LABYRINTH	H.	Longing
T - 9. RENDERED	I.	Disapproval
P - 10. FLACCID	J.	Leeway; freedom within regulations
U - 11. IMPALPABLE	K.	Ambition
M - 12. ELUDED	L.	Not subsiding; not becoming less
V - 13. VOWED	M.	Escaped from one's understanding
F - 14. SUBSIDED	N.	Maze
E - 15. DORMANT	O.	Found guilty or unfit
D - 16. DUPED	P.	Lacking firmness or muscle tone
J - 17. LATITUDE	Q.	Overbearingly; pressingly; urgently
O - 18. CONDEMNED	R.	Having uncontrolled emotions
K - 19. ASPIRATION	S.	Good
B - 20. GRATIFY	T.	Made; caused to be
H - 21. YEARNING	U.	Can't be grasped by touch or in the mind
A - 22. STAVE	V.	Promised
Q - 23. IMPERIOUSLY	W.	Can't be taken or sent back
S - 24. BENEVOLENT	X.	Not being able to escape from
Y - 25. ALIBI	Y.	An excuse; a way to prove one could not have committed a crime

Copyrighted

Native Son Vocabulary Magic Squares 1

Match the definition with the vocabulary word. Put your answers in the magic squares below. When your answers are correct, all columns and rows will add to the same number.

A. CONJECTURED
B. EBBED
C. BELLIGERENTLY
D. MITIGATING
E. SULLEN
F. IRKED
G. TAUT
H. BENEVOLENT
I. DUPED
J. ANARCHIST
K. ALIBI
L. EXHORTED
M. RENDERED
N. IMPELLED
O. CONSENTED
P. INARTICULATE

1. Good
2. Thought; came to a conclusion based on present evidence
3. Flowed away from
4. Tight; tense
5. One who is against all forms of government
6. Agreed
7. Wordless; speechless
8. Deceived; made to look foolish
9. An excuse; a way to prove one could not have committed a crime
10. Motivated; had the feeling of needing to do something
11. Made; caused to be
12. Urged through arguments or appeals
13. Sulky
14. Making more moderate
15. Hostilely
16. Irritated; bothered

A=	B=	C=	D=
E=	F=	G=	H=
I=	J=	K=	L=
M=	N=	O=	P=

Native Son Vocabulary Magic Squares 1 Answer Key

Match the definition with the vocabulary word. Put your answers in the magic squares below. When your answers are correct, all columns and rows will add to the same number.

A. CONJECTURED
B. EBBED
C. BELLIGERENTLY
D. MITIGATING
E. SULLEN
F. IRKED
G. TAUT
H. BENEVOLENT
I. DUPED
J. ANARCHIST
K. ALIBI
L. EXHORTED
M. RENDERED
N. IMPELLED
O. CONSENTED
P. INARTICULATE

1. Good
2. Thought; came to a conclusion based on present evidence
3. Flowed away from
4. Tight; tense
5. One who is against all forms of government
6. Agreed
7. Wordless; speechless
8. Deceived; made to look foolish
9. An excuse; a way to prove one could not have committed a crime
10. Motivated; had the feeling of needing to do something
11. Made; caused to be
12. Urged through arguments or appeals
13. Sulky
14. Making more moderate
15. Hostilely
16. Irritated; bothered

A=2	B=3	C=15	D=14
E=13	F=16	G=4	H=1
I=8	J=5	K=9	L=12
M=11	N=10	O=6	P=7

Native Son Vocabulary Magic Squares 2

Match the definition with the vocabulary word. Put your answers in the magic squares below. When your answers are correct, all columns and rows will add to the same number.

A. CONSENTED
B. QUEER
C. IRREVOCABLE
D. FUTILE
E. ABSTRACTEDLY
F. PEEVED
G. LULLED
H. IMPLICATE
I. LABYRINTH
J. LATITUDE
K. ARRAIGNMENT
L. REPROACH
M. UNABATING
N. INARTICULATE
O. FLACCID
P. BELLIGERENTLY

1. Connect incriminatingly
2. Not subsiding; not becoming less
3. Strange
4. Court proceeding in which accused persons answer the charges brought against them
5. Leeway; freedom within regulations
6. Can't be taken or sent back
7. Hostilely
8. In a manner apart from the situation
9. Lacking firmness or muscle tone
10. Vexed; angry
11. Maze
12. Useless
13. Agreed
14. Disapproval
15. Calmed
16. Wordless; speechless

A=	B=	C=	D=
E=	F=	G=	H=
I=	J=	K=	L=
M=	N=	O=	P=

Native Son Vocabulary Magic Squares 2 Answer Key

Match the definition with the vocabulary word. Put your answers in the magic squares below. When your answers are correct, all columns and rows will add to the same number.

A. CONSENTED
B. QUEER
C. IRREVOCABLE
D. FUTILE
E. ABSTRACTEDLY
F. PEEVED
G. LULLED
H. IMPLICATE
I. LABYRINTH
J. LATITUDE
K. ARRAIGNMENT
L. REPROACH
M. UNABATING
N. INARTICULATE
O. FLACCID
P. BELLIGERENTLY

1. Connect incriminatingly
2. Not subsiding; not becoming less
3. Strange
4. Court proceeding in which accused persons answer the charges brought against them
5. Leeway; freedom within regulations
6. Can't be taken or sent back
7. Hostilely
8. In a manner apart from the situation
9. Lacking firmness or muscle tone
10. Vexed; angry
11. Maze
12. Useless
13. Agreed
14. Disapproval
15. Calmed
16. Wordless; speechless

A=13	B=3	C=6	D=12
E=8	F=10	G=15	H=1
I=11	J=5	K=4	L=14
M=2	N=16	O=9	P=7

Native Son Vocabulary Magic Squares 3

Match the definition with the vocabulary word. Put your answers in the magic squares below. When your answers are correct, all columns and rows will add to the same number.

A. CONJECTURED
B. VOWED
C. FUTILE
D. SUBSIDED
E. IMPERIOUSLY
F. INARTICULATE
G. PEEVED
H. ARDENTLY
I. HYSTERICAL
J. ELUDED
K. GRATIFY
L. ATONE
M. CONTAGION
N. LINGERING
O. ASPIRATION
P. YEARNING

1. Ambition
2. Quieted; settled
3. Escaped from one's understanding
4. Overbearingly; pressingly; urgently
5. Having uncontrolled emotions
6. Wordless; speechless
7. Longing
8. Useless
9. Enthusiastically; fervently
10. Satisfy; indulge
11. Thought; came to a conclusion based on present evidence
12. Remaining, as though reluctant to leave
13. Promised
14. Easily transmitted disease
15. Vexed; angry
16. Make up for; make amends for

A=	B=	C=	D=
E=	F=	G=	H=
I=	J=	K=	L=
M=	N=	O=	P=

Native Son Vocabulary Magic Squares 3 Answer Key

Match the definition with the vocabulary word. Put your answers in the magic squares below. When your answers are correct, all columns and rows will add to the same number.

A. CONJECTURED
B. VOWED
C. FUTILE
D. SUBSIDED
E. IMPERIOUSLY
F. INARTICULATE
G. PEEVED
H. ARDENTLY
I. HYSTERICAL
J. ELUDED
K. GRATIFY
L. ATONE
M. CONTAGION
N. LINGERING
O. ASPIRATION
P. YEARNING

1. Ambition
2. Quieted; settled
3. Escaped from one's understanding
4. Overbearingly; pressingly; urgently
5. Having uncontrolled emotions
6. Wordless; speechless
7. Longing
8. Useless
9. Enthusiastically; fervently
10. Satisfy; indulge
11. Thought; came to a conclusion based on present evidence
12. Remaining, as though reluctant to leave
13. Promised
14. Easily transmitted disease
15. Vexed; angry
16. Make up for; make amends for

A=11	B=13	C=8	D=2
E=4	F=6	G=15	H=9
I=5	J=3	K=10	L=16
M=14	N=12	O=1	P=7

Copyrighted

Native Son Vocabulary Magic Squares 4

Match the definition with the vocabulary word. Put your answers in the magic squares below. When your answers are correct, all columns and rows will add to the same number.

A. ATONE
B. IRREVOCABLE
C. FUTILE
D. CONJECTURED
E. SUCCUMB
F. LINGERING
G. IRKED
H. IMPELLED
I. VOWED
J. CONDEMNED
K. AWE
L. VENUE
M. ANARCHIST
N. ALIBI
O. PREMEDITATION
P. IMPLICATE

1. Can't be taken or sent back
2. Irritated; bothered
3. Mixed emotion of reverence, respect, and dread
4. An excuse; a way to prove one could not have committed a crime
5. One who is against all forms of government
6. Location where a trial is held
7. Motivated; had the feeling of needing to do something
8. Make up for; make amends for
9. Connect incriminatingly
10. Promised
11. Give in; come under the influence of
12. Thought; came to a conclusion based on present evidence
13. Useless
14. Remaining, as though reluctant to leave
15. Found guilty or unfit
16. Planning beforehand

A=	B=	C=	D=
E=	F=	G=	H=
I=	J=	K=	L=
M=	N=	O=	P=

Native Son Vocabulary Magic Squares 4 Answer Key

Match the definition with the vocabulary word. Put your answers in the magic squares below. When your answers are correct, all columns and rows will add to the same number.

A. ATONE
B. IRREVOCABLE
C. FUTILE
D. CONJECTURED
E. SUCCUMB
F. LINGERING
G. IRKED
H. IMPELLED
I. VOWED
J. CONDEMNED
K. AWE
L. VENUE
M. ANARCHIST
N. ALIBI
O. PREMEDITATION
P. IMPLICATE

1. Can't be taken or sent back
2. Irritated; bothered
3. Mixed emotion of reverence, respect, and dread
4. An excuse; a way to prove one could not have committed a crime
5. One who is against all forms of government
6. Location where a trial is held
7. Motivated; had the feeling of needing to do something
8. Make up for; make amends for
9. Connect incriminatingly
10. Promised
11. Give in; come under the influence of
12. Thought; came to a conclusion based on present evidence
13. Useless
14. Remaining, as though reluctant to leave
15. Found guilty or unfit
16. Planning beforehand

A=8	B=1	C=13	D=12
E=11	F=14	G=2	H=7
I=10	J=15	K=3	L=6
M=5	N=4	O=16	P=9

Native Son Vocabulary Word Search 1

```
E G R A T I F Y L U L L E D S U R L Y
L X B Q N P L B V G N N S Z P E E V H
I Y H Y A Q A E L I O E R U N V E S T
T T S O R B C C N T G B T D C L U S N
U A A R R I L A D S I E H B C Q G I
F N N E A T R F I R U R L A I J U H R
B A C L I M E D R H E R C A G C G M Y
C R T B G W T D K D J O E G N J A B B
Y C I A N E S P E E V E D F I T V L A
M H O P M S Y Z D E T F L L T I E Y L
D I N L E L H N R A C A Q A A M N S W
D S M A N U V R L C C X R T B P U G M
G T M P T P I U G C J E C E A E E S I
N Y V M L M C M I O P W O N N L U Y T
I A L I B I L D O R M A N T U L S E I
R M B K T L C G O D W F S D L E L A G
E G P R S E L A T I O N E E Q D V R A
G T A U N P C G T L V D N Y C O S N T
N N A M T H D U P E D X T J W Z J I I
I M F U S E M O R A S S E E J R M N N
L A T I T U D E V A T S D E B B E G G
```

Agreed (9)
Agreement (6)
An excuse; a way to prove one could not have committed a crime (5)
Approve (8)
Asleep; inactive (7)
Attributed; credited (7)
Bad-humored; gruff (5)
Calmed (6)
Can't be grasped by touch or in the mind (10)
Can't be taken or sent back (11)
Carry on through hardships (6)
Connect incriminatingly (9)
Court proceeding in which accused persons answer the charges brought against them (11)
Deceived; made to look foolish (5)
Disapproval (8)
Dormant; present but not active (6)
Escaped from one's understanding (6)
Feeling of extreme happiness or pleasure (7)
Flowed away from (5)
Give in; come under the influence of (7)
Having uncontrolled emotions (10)
Inclination; motivating force (7)
Irritated; bothered (5)
Lacking firmness or muscle tone (7)
Leeway; freedom within regulations (8)

Location where a trial is held (5)
Longing (8)
Made; caused to be (8)
Make up for; make amends for (5)
Making more moderate (10)
Maze (9)
Mixed emotion of reverence, respect, and dread (3)
Motivated; had the feeling of needing to do something (8)
Not subsiding; not becoming less (9)
One who is against all forms of government (9)
People who take the law into their own hands (10)
Promised (5)
Put off; postpone (5)
Remaining, as though reluctant to leave (9)
Satisfy; indulge (7)
Something that hinders, engulfs, or overwhelms (6)
Strange (5)
Sulky (6)
Tight; tense (4)
Urged through arguments or appeals (8)
Useless (6)
Vexed; angry (6)
Wordless; speechless (12)
Wrong; not within accepted guidelines (9)

Native Son Vocabulary Word Search 1 Answer Key

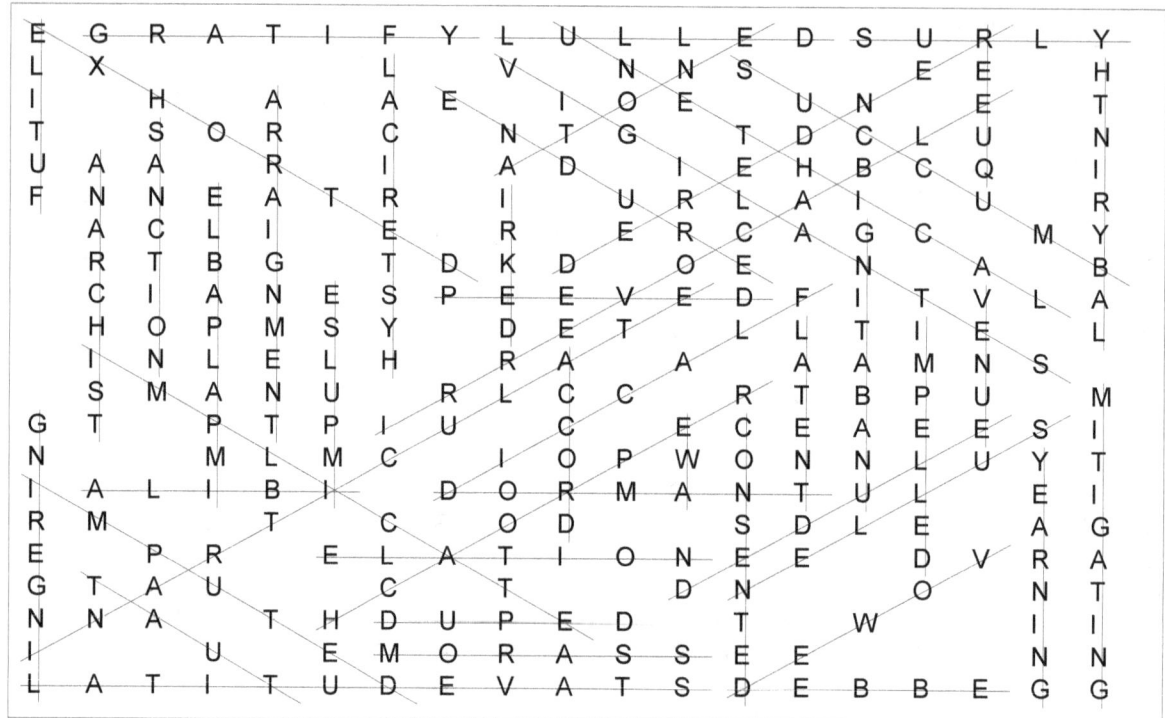

Agreed (9)
Agreement (6)
An excuse; a way to prove one could not have committed a crime (5)
Approve (8)
Asleep; inactive (7)
Attributed; credited (7)
Bad-humored; gruff (5)
Calmed (6)
Can't be grasped by touch or in the mind (10)
Can't be taken or sent back (11)
Carry on through hardships (6)
Connect incriminatingly (9)
Court proceeding in which accused persons answer the charges brought against them (11)
Deceived; made to look foolish (5)
Disapproval (8)
Dormant; present but not active (6)
Escaped from one's understanding (6)
Feeling of extreme happiness or pleasure (7)
Flowed away from (5)
Give in; come under the influence of (7)
Having uncontrolled emotions (10)
Inclination; motivating force (7)
Irritated; bothered (5)
Lacking firmness or muscle tone (7)
Leeway; freedom within regulations (8)

Location where a trial is held (5)
Longing (8)
Made; caused to be (8)
Make up for; make amends for (5)
Making more moderate (10)
Maze (9)
Mixed emotion of reverence, respect, and dread (3)
Motivated; had the feeling of needing to do something (8)
Not subsiding; not becoming less (9)
One who is against all forms of government (9)
People who take the law into their own hands (10)
Promised (5)
Put off; postpone (5)
Remaining, as though reluctant to leave (9)
Satisfy; indulge (7)
Something that hinders, engulfs, or overwhelms (6)
Strange (5)
Sulky (6)
Tight; tense (4)
Urged through arguments or appeals (8)
Useless (6)
Vexed; angry (6)
Wordless; speechless (12)
Wrong; not within accepted guidelines (9)

Native Son Vocabulary Word Search 2

```
D O R M A N T C N G S U L L E N H N I
E B V P C K S O I M P U L S E J T O M
L E B L W V I N Y M F C C W M D N I P
L N L G S T H J E F P K B C P S I G E
U E D R A D C E A F Y E E J U M R A R
L V M L N X R C R W U B L M P M Y T I
A O E T C C A T N Q R T L L N P B N O
R L J V T F N U I V C T I C E D A O U
R E V P I A A R N H I C G L E D L C S
A N F R O H R E G M A I E K E Q L O L
I T B L N B R D P T N B R Z G S A N Y
G K Q G A K A U E D M I E V T C T D T
N H U B F C T F E N D L N E Q R I E J
M Q E R C E C L V A T A T N R T T M E
E O E O D L I I E W D L L U N G U N V
N V R S U B S I D E D T Y E L U D E D
T D S A L V T J X L U L T B Y U E D S
H T W E S B A M F A R A R B R G W D M
D U P E D S V P T U L X D E X Z O J Z
A T O N E D E B S J R K S D L C V K K
L I N G E R I N G N I T A G I T I M Z
```

Agreement (6)
An excuse; a way to prove one could not have committed a crime (5)
Approve (8)
Asleep; inactive (7)
Attributed; credited (7)
Bad-humored; gruff (5)
Calmed (6)
Carry on through hardships (6)
Connect incriminatingly (9)
Court proceeding in which accused persons answer the charges brought against them (11)
Deceived; made to look foolish (5)
Dormant; present but not active (6)
Easily transmitted disease (9)
Enthusiastically; fervently (8)
Escaped from one's understanding (6)
Feeling of extreme happiness or pleasure (7)
Flowed away from (5)
Found guilty or unfit (9)
Give in; come under the influence of (7)
Good (10)
Hostilely (13)
Inclination; motivating force (7)
Irritated; bothered (5)
Lacking firmness or muscle tone (7)
Leeway; freedom within regulations (8)

Location where a trial is held (5)
Longing (8)
Make up for; make amends for (5)
Making more moderate (10)
Maze (9)
Mixed emotion of reverence, respect, and dread (3)
Motivated; had the feeling of needing to do something (8)
One who is against all forms of government (9)
Overbearingly; pressingly; urgently (11)
Permanent (9)
Promised (5)
Put off; postpone (5)
Quieted; settled (8)
Remaining, as though reluctant to leave (9)
Something that hinders, engulfs, or overwhelms (6)
Strange (5)
Sulky (6)
Thought; came to a conclusion based on present evidence (11)
Tight; tense (4)
Useless (6)
Vexed; angry (6)

Native Son Vocabulary Word Search 2 Answer Key

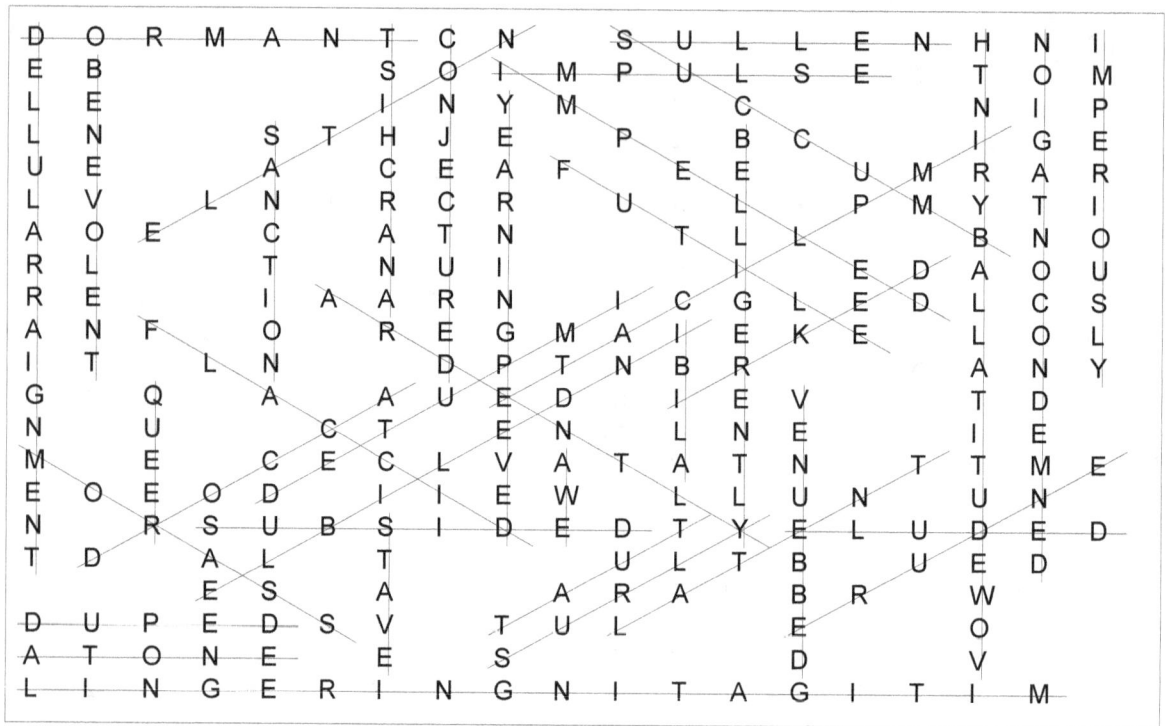

Agreement (6)
An excuse; a way to prove one could not have committed a crime (5)
Approve (8)
Asleep; inactive (7)
Attributed; credited (7)
Bad-humored; gruff (5)
Calmed (6)
Carry on through hardships (6)
Connect incriminatingly (9)
Court proceeding in which accused persons answer the charges brought against them (11)
Deceived; made to look foolish (5)
Dormant; present but not active (6)
Easily transmitted disease (9)
Enthusiastically; fervently (8)
Escaped from one's understanding (6)
Feeling of extreme happiness or pleasure (7)
Flowed away from (5)
Found guilty or unfit (9)
Give in; come under the influence of (7)
Good (10)
Hostilely (13)
Inclination; motivating force (7)
Irritated; bothered (5)
Lacking firmness or muscle tone (7)
Leeway; freedom within regulations (8)

Location where a trial is held (5)
Longing (8)
Make up for; make amends for (5)
Making more moderate (10)
Maze (9)
Mixed emotion of reverence, respect, and dread (3)
Motivated; had the feeling of needing to do something (8)
One who is against all forms of government (9)
Overbearingly; pressingly; urgently (11)
Permanent (9)
Promised (5)
Put off; postpone (5)
Quieted; settled (8)
Remaining, as though reluctant to leave (9)
Something that hinders, engulfs, or overwhelms (6)
Strange (5)
Sulky (6)
Thought; came to a conclusion based on present evidence (11)
Tight; tense (4)
Useless (6)
Vexed; angry (6)

Native Son Vocabulary Word Search 3

```
P Z W S N S X T E F I N D E L I B L E
T R L L S W G L E T Y E J K A F S E N
F V E A T J U A R A P U B E C T L Z N
C N R M D D S T U U F N L R X I O G Y
C O N D E M N E D T S A N C T I O N Y
M I N D B D W N T T B C U D M W I E Y
C T I J B A I T E I S A F C R P B T Y
O A G M E D Y T O Z U T V L O E G A W
N R R M P C J N A Q B I E A X R X G Y
S I N D M U T N B T S N N B K I D I V
E P H C E G T U F U I G U Y Q O M T V
N S G R E N D E R E D O E R L U D I Z
T A T X A I T L D E E J N I A S E M R
E B C M C D Y L D S D D S N T L K E R
D Y R C N O Q E Y U E S T T I Y R D R
S O A T D B V W T L S U A H T X I V H
D L L N N E Q L L L C V V U N O S L
F Y I L E R P U N E U C E X D W Q N D
B P B P Q O L R Y N P U W B B D N G
L N I S G F Q Y K V M M D D N D J K Y
R E P R O A C H C D I B G R A T I F Y
```

ACCORD	ELATION	LABYRINTH	STAVE
ALIBI	ELUDED	LATENT	SUBSIDED
ARDENTLY	ENDURE	LATITUDE	SUCCUMB
ASPIRATION	FLACCID	LULLED	SULLEN
ATONE	FOREBODING	MITIGATING	SURLY
AWE	FUTILE	MORASS	TAUT
CONDEMNED	GRATIFY	PEEVED	UNABATING
CONJECTURED	IMPERIOUSLY	PREMEDITATION	VENUE
CONSENTED	IMPULSE	QUEER	VOWED
DORMANT	IMPUTED	RENDERED	
DUPED	INDELIBLE	REPROACH	
EBBED	IRKED	SANCTION	

Native Son Vocabulary Word Search 3 Answer Key

ACCORD	ELATION	LABYRINTH	STAVE
ALIBI	ELUDED	LATENT	SUBSIDED
ARDENTLY	ENDURE	LATITUDE	SUCCUMB
ASPIRATION	FLACCID	LULLED	SULLEN
ATONE	FOREBODING	MITIGATING	SURLY
AWE	FUTILE	MORASS	TAUT
CONDEMNED	GRATIFY	PEEVED	UNABATING
CONJECTURED	IMPERIOUSLY	PREMEDITATION	VENUE
CONSENTED	IMPULSE	QUEER	VOWED
DORMANT	IMPUTED	RENDERED	
DUPED	INDELIBLE	REPROACH	
EBBED	IRKED	SANCTION	

Native Son Vocabulary Word Search 4

```
L A B Y R I N T H Y S T E R I C A L C
I M P A L P A B L E B N Z T O I G A O
N Y J V S E I Z A V X A Z N M N R T N
G M I R K E D M O C W M T C E D A I D
E D O P X V D W P P C R T R V E T T E
R D B R G E E S T U I O U E A L I U M
I B L T A D D U S T T D R N T I F D N
N F U M S S I C E D N E M D S B Y E E
G C L Q A F S C A E A G D E W L C U D
P A L A N T B U B T N N F R Q E O N I
F U E A C M U M S R A M U E J B N E N
G G D R T C S B T O R S T D B B T T A
N M X D I Y I N R H C E I N X E A H R
I E N E O Q E D A X H T L S S D G I T
D N G N N T U S C E I N E U E D I C I
O T A T A R N E T N S A R D L T O A C
B E L L I G E R E N T L Y G U A N L U
E D F Y I R V L D R Y I S A D P W R L
R R T N S B L Q L C F G T Z E V E E A
O P X Y S U I Q Y R M I R K D T D D T
F N J Z S A T O N E G V I M P U L S E
```

ABSTRACTEDLY	DUPED	INARTICULATE	STAVE
ACCORD	EBBED	INDELIBLE	SUBSIDED
ALIBI	ELUDED	IRKED	SUCCUMB
ANARCHIST	ENDURE	LABYRINTH	SULLEN
ARDENTLY	EXHORTED	LATENT	SURLY
ATONE	FLACCID	LATITUDE	TAUT
AUGMENTED	FOREBODING	LINGERING	UNETHICAL
AWE	FUTILE	LULLED	VENUE
BELLIGERENTLY	GRATIFY	MORASS	VIGILANTES
CONDEMNED	HYSTERICAL	PEEVED	VOWED
CONTAGION	IMPALPABLE	QUEER	
CONTRITE	IMPULSE	RENDERED	
DORMANT	IMPUTED	SANCTION	

Native Son Vocabulary Word Search 4 Answer Key

```
L  A  B  Y  R  I  N  T  H  Y  S  T  E  R  I  C  A  L        C
I  M  P  A  L  P  A  B  L  E     N        O     I  G  R  A  O
N           E  I     A  V        N        N     N  R  A  T  N
G  M  I  R  K  E  D  M  O  C     M        E     D  A  T  I  D
E     O     E  V  D  W  P  U  C  R        V     E  T  I  T  E
R     R     V  E  S  S  U  T  O  U        A     L  I  T  U  M
I     L     E  D  D  I  C  T  N  R        T     I  F  U  D  N
N  F  U     D  S  U  C  C  U  M  B     D  S     B  Y  D  E  E
G  A  L        A  N  B  U  A  B  S        F     B     E        D
   U  L  E     A  C  S  M  B  S  T        U     E     U        I
G  G  E  D     R  T  I  S  T  T  R        T     D     N        N
N  M  N     C  D  I  O  N  R  R  A        I     C     E        A
I  E  T     I  E  O  N  D  A  A  C        L     T     T        R
D  N     A  T  N  A     E  C  X  H        E     A     H        T
O  T     L  B  E  L  L  I  G  E  R  E  N  T     P     I        I
B  E     L  Y  I  V  E  R  E  N  T  L  Y  A     E     C        C
E  D        B  U  L  L  Y  D  R  L  Y  G  T        E  A        U
R              S  A  T  O  N  E        V  I  M  P  U  L  S  E
O
F
```

ABSTRACTEDLY   DUPED   INARTICULATE   STAVE

ACCORD   EBBED   INDELIBLE   SUBSIDED

ALIBI   ELUDED   IRKED   SUCCUMB

ANARCHIST   ENDURE   LABYRINTH   SULLEN

ARDENTLY   EXHORTED   LATENT   SURLY

ATONE   FLACCID   LATITUDE   TAUT

AUGMENTED   FOREBODING   LINGERING   UNETHICAL

AWE   FUTILE   LULLED   VENUE

BELLIGERENTLY   GRATIFY   MORASS   VIGILANTES

CONDEMNED   HYSTERICAL   PEEVED   VOWED

CONTAGION   IMPALPABLE   QUEER

CONTRITE   IMPULSE   RENDERED

DORMANT   IMPUTED   SANCTION

Native Son Vocabulary Crossword 1

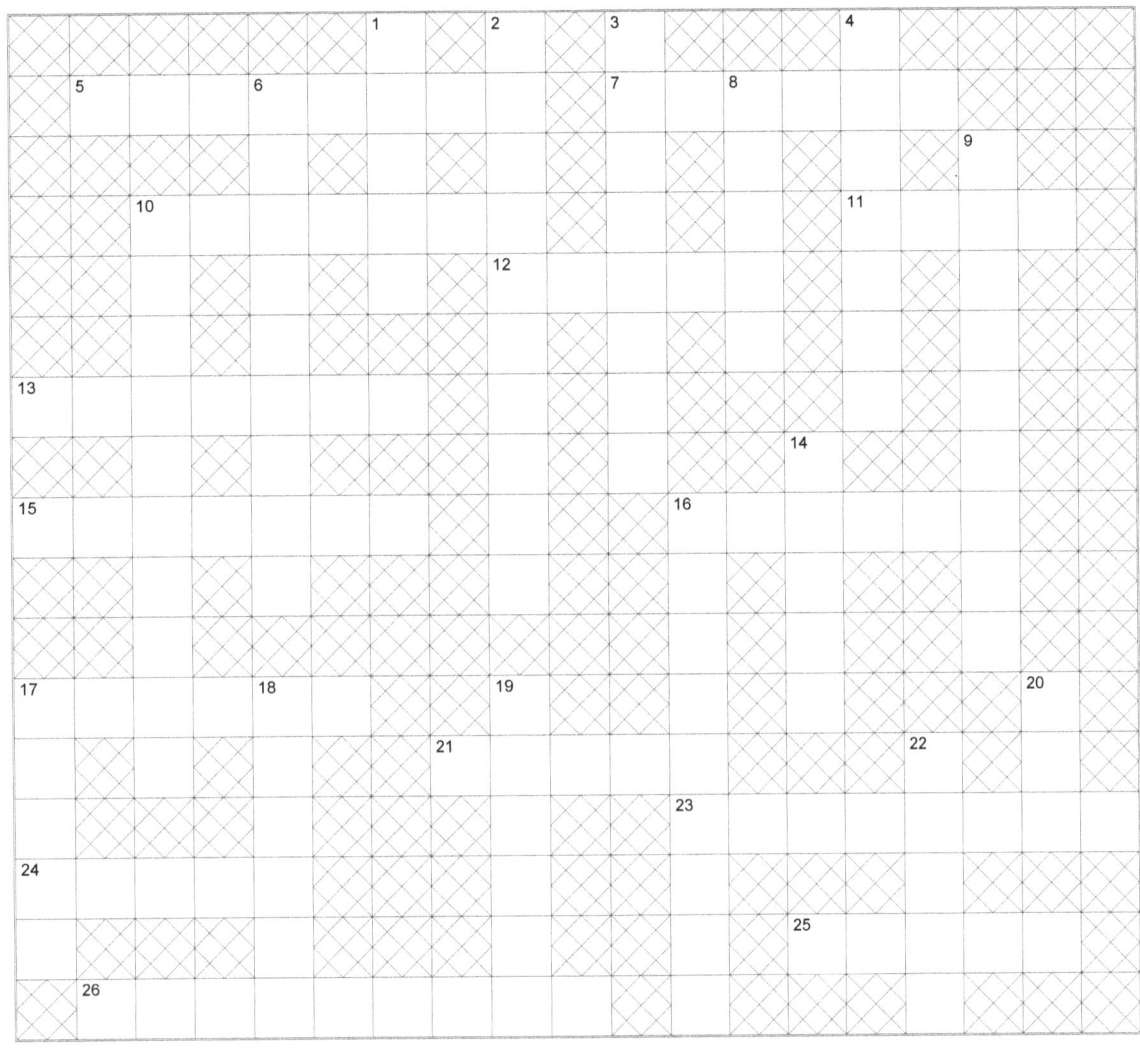

Across
5. Leeway; freedom within regulations
7. Carry on through hardships
10. Inclination; motivating force
11. Tight; tense
12. Location where a trial is held
13. Lacking firmness or muscle tone
15. Attributed; credited
16. Dormant; present but not active
17. Sulky
21. Strange
23. Motivated; had the feeling of needing to do something
24. Promised
25. Flowed away from
26. Found guilty or unfit

Down
1. Bad-humored; gruff
2. Good
3. Longing
4. Satisfy; indulge
6. Connect incriminatingly
8. Deceived; made to look foolish
9. Added to; supplemented
10. Can't be grasped by touch or in the mind
14. Make up for; make amends for
16. Maze
17. Put off; postpone
18. Escaped from one's understanding
19. Useless
20. Mixed emotion of reverence, respect, and dread
22. An excuse; a way to prove one could not have committed a crime

Native Son Vocabulary Crossword 1 Answer Key

						¹S		²B		³Y			⁴G		
	⁵L	A	T	⁶I	T	U	D	E		⁷E	N	⁸D	U	R	E
				M		R		N		A		U	A		⁹A
		¹⁰I	M	P	U	L	S	E		R		P	¹¹T	A	U	T
		M		L		Y		¹²V	E	N	U	E		I		G
		P		I				O		I		D		F		M
	¹³F	L	A	C	C	I	D			L		N			Y		E
		L		A					L		G		¹⁴A		N
¹⁵I	M	P	U	T	E	D			¹⁶L	A	T	E	N	T
		A		E					T		A		O		E
		B						B		N		D	
¹⁷S	U	L	L	¹⁸E	N		¹⁹F		Y		E			²⁰A
T		E		L		²¹Q	U	E	E	R			²²A		W
A				U		T			²³I	M	P	E	L	L	E	D
²⁴V	O	W	E	D		I			N				I	
E				E		L			T		²⁵E	B	B	E	D
		²⁶C	O	N	D	E	M	N	E	D		H			I

Across
5. Leeway; freedom within regulations
7. Carry on through hardships
10. Inclination; motivating force
11. Tight; tense
12. Location where a trial is held
13. Lacking firmness or muscle tone
15. Attributed; credited
16. Dormant; present but not active
17. Sulky
21. Strange
23. Motivated; had the feeling of needing to do something
24. Promised
25. Flowed away from
26. Found guilty or unfit

Down
1. Bad-humored; gruff
2. Good
3. Longing
4. Satisfy; indulge
6. Connect incriminatingly
8. Deceived; made to look foolish
9. Added to; supplemented
10. Can't be grasped by touch or in the mind
14. Make up for; make amends for
16. Maze
17. Put off; postpone
18. Escaped from one's understanding
19. Useless
20. Mixed emotion of reverence, respect, and dread
22. An excuse; a way to prove one could not have committed a crime

Native Son Vocabulary Crossword 2

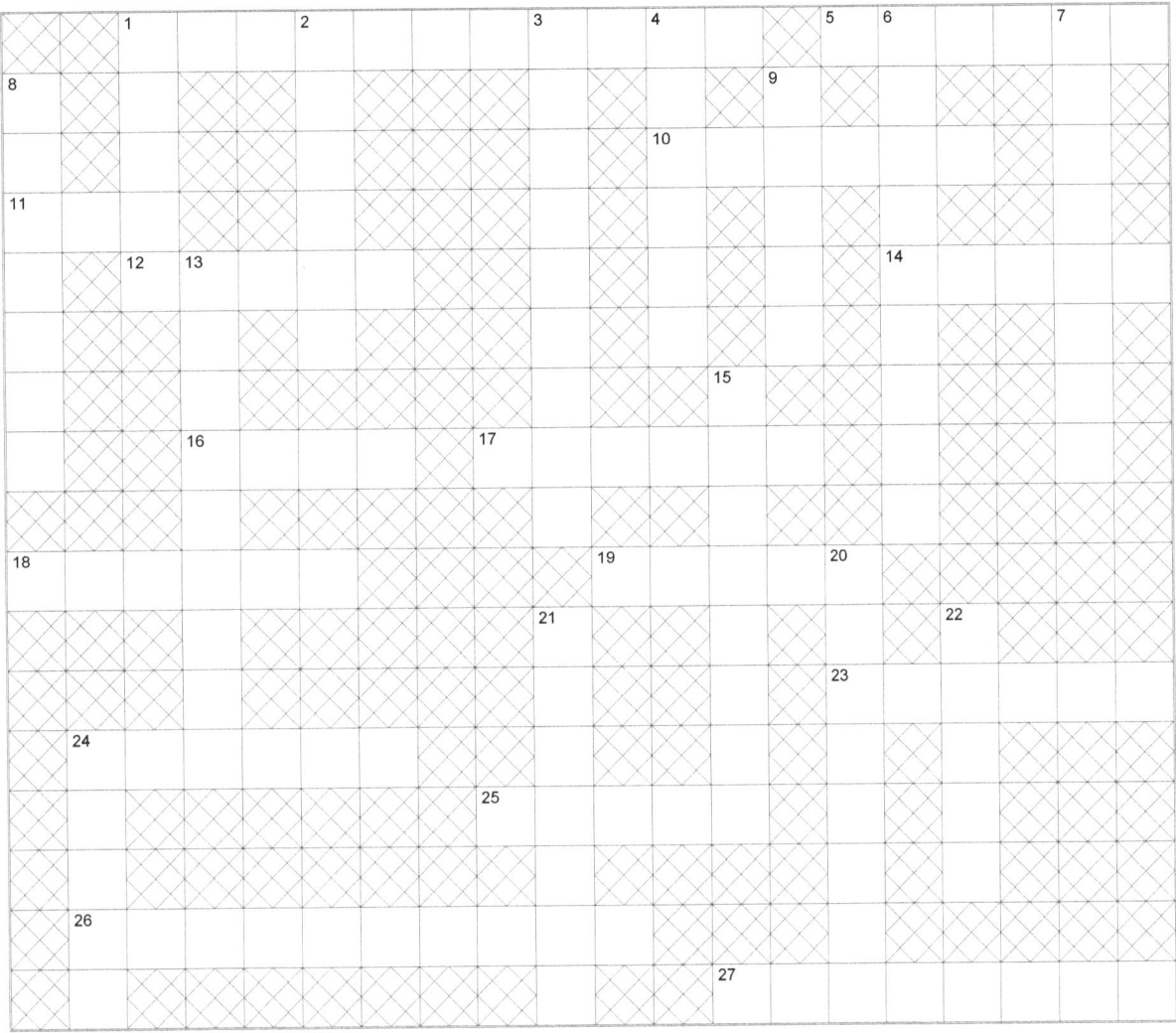

Across
1. Overbearingly; pressingly; urgently
5. Agreement
10. Dormant; present but not active
11. Mixed emotion of reverence, respect, and dread
12. Deceived; made to look foolish
14. Flowed away from
16. Tight; tense
17. Carry on through hardships
18. Useless
19. Strange
23. Vexed; angry
24. Sulky
25. Bad-humored; gruff
26. People who take the law into their own hands
27. Urged through arguments or appeals

Down
1. Irritated; bothered
2. Escaped from one's understanding
3. Not subsiding; not becoming less
4. Calmed
6. Found guilty or unfit
7. Made; caused to be
8. Satisfy; indulge
9. Make up for; make amends for
13. Wrong; not within accepted guidelines
15. Enthusiastically; fervently
20. Disapproval
21. Attributed; credited
22. Location where a trial is held
24. Put off; postpone

Native Son Vocabulary Crossword 2 Answer Key

Across
1. Overbearingly; pressingly; urgently
5. Agreement
10. Dormant; present but not active
11. Mixed emotion of reverence, respect, and dread
12. Deceived; made to look foolish
14. Flowed away from
16. Tight; tense
17. Carry on through hardships
18. Useless
19. Strange
23. Vexed; angry
24. Sulky
25. Bad-humored; gruff
26. People who take the law into their own hands
27. Urged through arguments or appeals

Down
1. Irritated; bothered
2. Escaped from one's understanding
3. Not subsiding; not becoming less
4. Calmed
6. Found guilty or unfit
7. Made; caused to be
8. Satisfy; indulge
9. Make up for; make amends for
13. Wrong; not within accepted guidelines
15. Enthusiastically; fervently
20. Disapproval
21. Attributed; credited
22. Location where a trial is held
24. Put off; postpone

Native Son Vocabulary Crossword 3

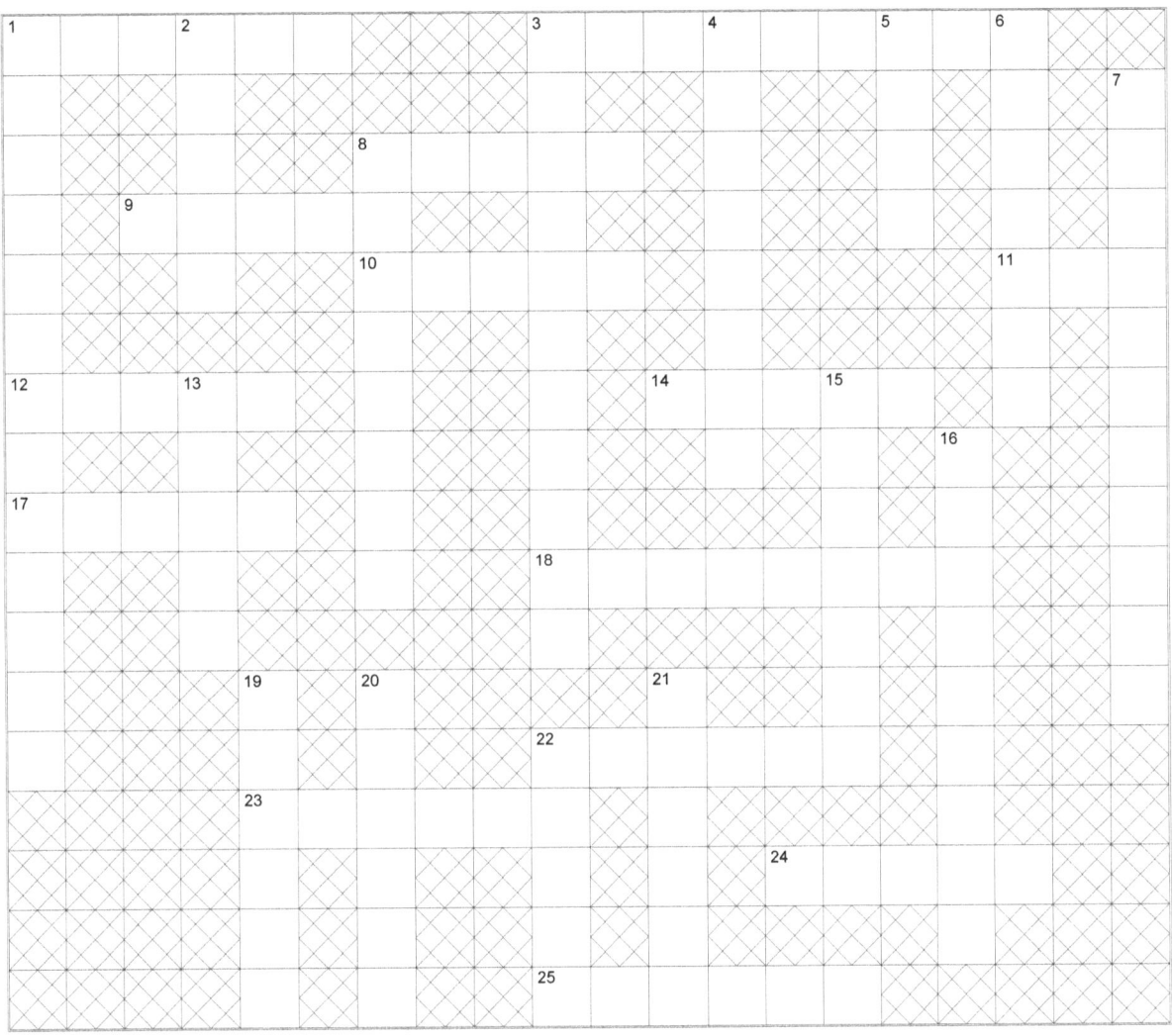

Across
1. Vexed; angry
3. Agreed
8. Make up for; make amends for
9. Strange
10. Deceived; made to look foolish
11. Mixed emotion of reverence, respect, and dread
12. Irritated; bothered
14. Promised
17. An excuse; a way to prove one could not have committed a crime
18. Urged through arguments or appeals
22. Sulky
23. Dormant; present but not active
24. Bad-humored; gruff
25. Carry on through hardships

Down
1. Planning beforehand
2. Location where a trial is held
3. Thought; came to a conclusion based on present evidence
4. Approve
5. Tight; tense
6. Asleep; inactive
7. Can't be taken or sent back
8. Enthusiastically; fervently
13. Flowed away from
15. Feeling of extreme happiness or pleasure
16. Permanent
19. Calmed
20. Useless
21. Escaped from one's understanding
22. Put off; postpone

Native Son Vocabulary Crossword 3 Answer Key

	1	2	3	4	5	6	7
1	P E E V E D		3 C O N S E N T E D				

Filled grid (row by row):

Row 1: P E E V E D . . C O N S E N T E D .
Row 2: R . . E . . . O . . A . . A . O . I
Row 3: E . . N . 8 A T O N E . A N . . U . R . R
Row 4: M . 9 Q U E E R . J . . . C . . T . . M . R
Row 5: E . . U . 10 D U P E D . T . . . . 11 A W E
Row 6: D . . E . . E . . C . . I . . . . N . V
Row 7: 12 I R 13 K E D . N . . T . 14 V O W 15 E D . T . O
Row 8: T . . B . . T . . U . . N . . L . 16 I . C
Row 9: 17 A L I B I . L . . R . . . . A . N . A
Row 10: T . . E . . Y . . 18 E X H O R T E D . B
Row 11: I . . D . . . . . D . . . . I . E . L
Row 12: O . . 19 L 20 F . . 21 E . . . O . L . E
Row 13: N . . U . U . . 22 S U L L E N . I . .
Row 14: . . 23 L A T E N T . U . . . B . .
Row 15: . . . L . I . . A . 24 S U R L Y .
Row 16: . . . E . L . . V . D . . E . . .
Row 17: . . . D . E . . 25 E N D U R E . .

Across
1. Vexed; angry
3. Agreed
8. Make up for; make amends for
9. Strange
10. Deceived; made to look foolish
11. Mixed emotion of reverence, respect, and dread
12. Irritated; bothered
14. Promised
17. An excuse; a way to prove one could not have committed a crime
18. Urged through arguments or appeals
22. Sulky
23. Dormant; present but not active
24. Bad-humored; gruff
25. Carry on through hardships

Down
1. Planning beforehand
2. Location where a trial is held
3. Thought; came to a conclusion based on present evidence
4. Approve
5. Tight; tense
6. Asleep; inactive
7. Can't be taken or sent back
8. Enthusiastically; fervently
13. Flowed away from
15. Feeling of extreme happiness or pleasure
16. Permanent
19. Calmed
20. Useless
21. Escaped from one's understanding
22. Put off; postpone

Native Son Vocabulary Crossword 4

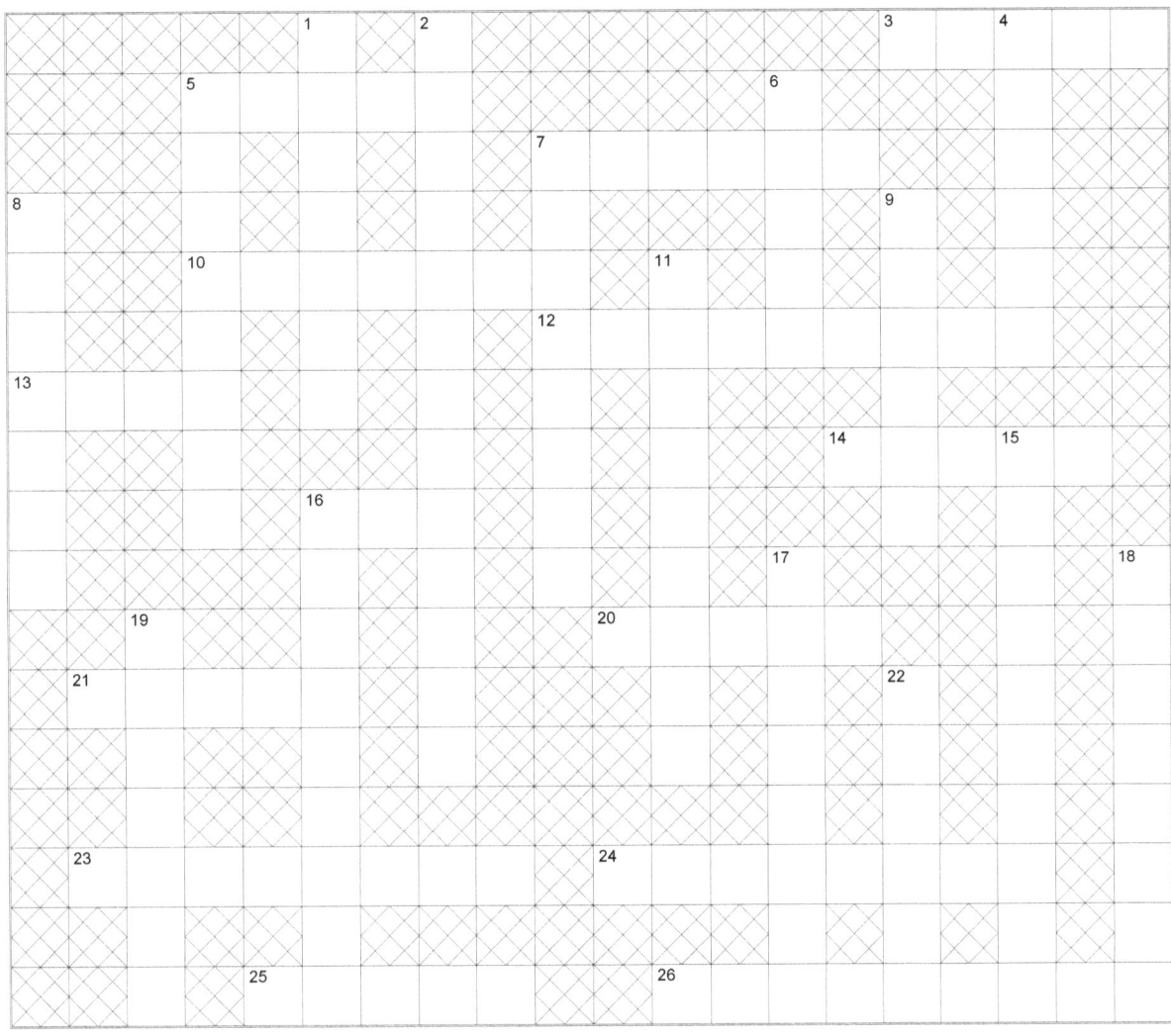

Across
3. Deceived; made to look foolish
5. Make up for; make amends for
7. Sulky
10. Feeling of extreme happiness or pleasure
12. Agreed
13. Tight; tense
14. An excuse; a way to prove one could not have committed a crime
16. Mixed emotion of reverence, respect, and dread
20. Flowed away from
21. Strange
23. Quieted; settled
24. Leeway; freedom within regulations
25. Put off; postpone
26. Added to; supplemented

Down
1. Asleep; inactive
2. Hostilely
4. Vexed; angry
5. Enthusiastically; fervently
6. Location where a trial is held
7. Approve
8. Satisfy; indulge
9. Useless
11. Permanent
15. Good
16. One who is against all forms of government
17. Longing
18. Motivated; had the feeling of needing to do something
19. Give in; come under the influence of
22. Carry on through hardships

Native Son Vocabulary Crossword 4 Answer Key

Across

3. Deceived; made to look foolish
5. Make up for; make amends for
7. Sulky
10. Feeling of extreme happiness or pleasure
12. Agreed
13. Tight; tense
14. An excuse; a way to prove one could not have committed a crime
16. Mixed emotion of reverence, respect, and dread
20. Flowed away from
21. Strange
23. Quieted; settled
24. Leeway; freedom within regulations
25. Put off; postpone
26. Added to; supplemented

Down

1. Asleep; inactive
2. Hostilely
4. Vexed; angry
5. Enthusiastically; fervently
6. Location where a trial is held
7. Approve
8. Satisfy; indulge
9. Useless
11. Permanent
15. Good
16. One who is against all forms of government
17. Longing
18. Motivated; had the feeling of needing to do something
19. Give in; come under the influence of
22. Carry on through hardships

Native Son Vocabulary Juggle Letters 1

1. LUSIYOMEIRP = 1. _____
   Overbearingly; pressingly; urgently

2. WEA = 2. _____
   Mixed emotion of reverence, respect, and dread

3. RENANYIG = 3. _____
   Longing

4. ANTIGNOCO = 4. _____
   Easily transmitted disease

5. DUDEEL = 5. _____
   Escaped from one's understanding

6. DOCRAC = 6. _____
   Agreement

7. EDNERDRE = 7. _____
   Made; caused to be

8. DEPDU = 8. _____
   Deceived; made to look foolish

9. EEURQ = 9. _____
   Strange

10. ORASSM = 10. _____
    Something that hinders, engulfs, or overwhelms

11. COATSNNI = 11. _____
    Approve

12. INATGNAUB = 12. _____
    Not subsiding; not becoming less

13. BEACVREORIL = 13. _____
    Can't be taken or sent back

14. OEWVD = 14. _____
    Promised

15. MNNDDOEEC = 15. _____
    Found guilty or unfit

Native Son Vocabulary Juggle Letters 1 Answer Key

1. LUSIYOMEIRP = 1. IMPERIOUSLY
   Overbearingly; pressingly; urgently

2. WEA = 2. AWE
   Mixed emotion of reverence, respect, and dread

3. RENANYIG = 3. YEARNING
   Longing

4. ANTIGNOCO = 4. CONTAGION
   Easily transmitted disease

5. DUDEEL = 5. ELUDED
   Escaped from one's understanding

6. DOCRAC = 6. ACCORD
   Agreement

7. EDNERDRE = 7. RENDERED
   Made; caused to be

8. DEPDU = 8. DUPED
   Deceived; made to look foolish

9. EEURQ = 9. QUEER
   Strange

10. ORASSM = 10. MORASS
    Something that hinders, engulfs, or overwhelms

11. COATSNNI = 11. SANCTION
    Approve

12. INATGNAUB = 12. UNABATING
    Not subsiding; not becoming less

13. BEACVREORIL = 13. IRREVOCABLE
    Can't be taken or sent back

14. OEWVD = 14. VOWED
    Promised

15. MNNDDOEEC = 15. CONDEMNED
    Found guilty or unfit

Native Son Vocabulary Juggle Letters 2

1. CENCUDRTEOJ = 1. _____
   Thought; came to a conclusion based on present evidence

2. TIRGFYA = 2. _____
   Satisfy; indulge

3. ANTPEOERIIMDT = 3. _____
   Planning beforehand

4. EEDHTRXO = 4. _____
   Urged through arguments or appeals

5. UATT = 5. _____
   Tight; tense

6. HERCAPRO = 6. _____
   Disapproval

7. ILAOETN = 7. _____
   Feeling of extreme happiness or pleasure

8. NEULLS = 8. _____
   Sulky

9. NREDDEER = 9. _____
   Made; caused to be

10. ACLNIIYBTRXE =10. _____
    Not being able to escape from

11. TRIBYHLAN =11. _____
    Maze

12. DTLEIATU =12. _____
    Leeway; freedom within regulations

13. INIGIATGMT =13. _____
    Making more moderate

14. NOOREGFIDB =14. _____
    Predicting something bad for the future

15. SOYIPRUMLEI =15. _____
    Overbearingly; pressingly; urgently

Native Son Vocabulary Juggle Letters 2 Answer Key

1. CENCUDRTEOJ = 1. CONJECTURED
   Thought; came to a conclusion based on present evidence

2. TIRGFYA = 2. GRATIFY
   Satisfy; indulge

3. ANTPEOERIIMDT = 3. PREMEDITATION
   Planning beforehand

4. EEDHTRXO = 4. EXHORTED
   Urged through arguments or appeals

5. UATT = 5. TAUT
   Tight; tense

6. HERCAPRO = 6. REPROACH
   Disapproval

7. ILAOETN = 7. ELATION
   Feeling of extreme happiness or pleasure

8. NEULLS = 8. SULLEN
   Sulky

9. NREDDEER = 9. RENDERED
   Made; caused to be

10. ACLNIIYBTRXE = 10. INEXTRICABLY
    Not being able to escape from

11. TRIBYHLAN = 11. LABYRINTH
    Maze

12. DTLEIATU = 12. LATITUDE
    Leeway; freedom within regulations

13. INIGIATGMT = 13. MITIGATING
    Making more moderate

14. NOOREGFIDB = 14. FOREBODING
    Predicting something bad for the future

15. SOYIPRUMLEI = 15. IMPERIOUSLY
    Overbearingly; pressingly; urgently

Native Son Vocabulary Juggle Letters 3

1. TCAEINLHU = 1. _____
   Wrong; not within accepted guidelines

2. OINOACNTG = 2. _____
   Easily transmitted disease

3. SSOARM = 3. _____
   Something that hinders, engulfs, or overwhelms

4. VAEST = 4. _____
   Put off; postpone

5. ATUT = 5. _____
   Tight; tense

6. EROAELCVRBI = 6. _____
   Can't be taken or sent back

7. IILAB = 7. _____
   An excuse; a way to prove one could not have committed a crime

8. LLGIEEYLNBETR = 8. _____
   Hostilely

9. CDAROC = 9. _____
   Agreement

10. PUDDE =10. _____
    Deceived; made to look foolish

11. RINLENIGG =11. _____
    Remaining, as though reluctant to leave

12. OGFDNEIORB =12. _____
    Predicting something bad for the future

13. EAW =13. _____
    Mixed emotion of reverence, respect, and dread

14. EISMLPU =14. _____
    Inclination; motivating force

15. EDLULL =15. _____
    Calmed

Native Son Vocabulary Juggle Letters 3 Answer Key

1. TCAEINLHU = 1. UNETHICAL
   Wrong; not within accepted guidelines

2. OINOACNTG = 2. CONTAGION
   Easily transmitted disease

3. SSOARM = 3. MORASS
   Something that hinders, engulfs, or overwhelms

4. VAEST = 4. STAVE
   Put off; postpone

5. ATUT = 5. TAUT
   Tight; tense

6. EROAELCVRBI = 6. IRREVOCABLE
   Can't be taken or sent back

7. IILAB = 7. ALIBI
   An excuse; a way to prove one could not have committed a crime

8. LLGIEEYLNBETR = 8. BELLIGERENTLY
   Hostilely

9. CDAROC = 9. ACCORD
   Agreement

10. PUDDE = 10. DUPED
    Deceived; made to look foolish

11. RINLENIGG = 11. LINGERING
    Remaining, as though reluctant to leave

12. OGFDNEIORB = 12. FOREBODING
    Predicting something bad for the future

13. EAW = 13. AWE
    Mixed emotion of reverence, respect, and dread

14. EISMLPU = 14. IMPULSE
    Inclination; motivating force

15. EDLULL = 15. LULLED
    Calmed

Native Son Vocabulary Juggle Letters 4

1. TTELAN = 1. _____
   Dormant; present but not active

2. WAE = 2. _____
   Mixed emotion of reverence, respect, and dread

3. DSTBRCATYLEA = 3. _____
   In a manner apart from the situation

4. EMULPSI = 4. _____
   Inclination; motivating force

5. ULDEED = 5. _____
   Escaped from one's understanding

6. DSDIBSEU = 6. _____
   Quieted; settled

7. NTITAMIIGG = 7. _____
   Making more moderate

8. LIUTFE = 8. _____
   Useless

9. EEMLILPD = 9. _____
   Motivated; had the feeling of needing to do something

10. RLYSU = 10. _____
    Bad-humored; gruff

11. CROEHRAP = 11. _____
    Disapproval

12. IDLBLEIEN = 12. _____
    Permanent

13. AELCNHTUI = 13. _____
    Wrong; not within accepted guidelines

14. TANCNSOI = 14. _____
    Approve

15. ONATE = 15. _____
    Make up for; make amends for

Native Son Vocabulary Juggle Letters 4 Answer Key

1. TTELAN = 1. LATENT
Dormant; present but not active

2. WAE = 2. AWE
Mixed emotion of reverence, respect, and dread

3. DSTBRCATYLEA = 3. ABSTRACTEDLY
In a manner apart from the situation

4. EMULPSI = 4. IMPULSE
Inclination; motivating force

5. ULDEED = 5. ELUDED
Escaped from one's understanding

6. DSDIBSEU = 6. SUBSIDED
Quieted; settled

7. NTITAMIIGG = 7. MITIGATING
Making more moderate

8. LIUTFE = 8. FUTILE
Useless

9. EEMLILPD = 9. IMPELLED
Motivated; had the feeling of needing to do something

10. RLYSU =10. SURLY
Bad-humored; gruff

11. CROEHRAP =11. REPROACH
Disapproval

12. IDLBLEIEN =12. INDELIBLE
Permanent

13. AELCNHTUI =13. UNETHICAL
Wrong; not within accepted guidelines

14. TANCNSOI =14. SANCTION
Approve

15. ONATE =15. ATONE
Make up for; make amends for

ABSTRACTEDLY	In a manner apart from the situation
ACCORD	Agreement
ALIBI	An excuse; a way to prove one could not have committed a crime
ANARCHIST	One who is against all forms of government
APPREHENSIVELY	Anxiously; fearfully
ARDENTLY	Enthusiastically; fervently

ARRAIGNMENT	Court proceeding in which accused persons answer the charges brought against them
ASPIRATION	Ambition
ATONE	Make up for; make amends for
AUGMENTED	Added to; supplemented
AWE	Mixed emotion of reverence, respect, and dread
BELLIGERENTLY	Hostilely

BENEVOLENT	Good
CONDEMNED	Found guilty or unfit
CONJECTURED	Thought; came to a conclusion based on present evidence
CONSENTED	Agreed
CONTAGION	Easily transmitted disease
CONTRITE	Sorry

DORMANT	Asleep; inactive
DUPED	Deceived; made to look foolish
EBBED	Flowed away from
ELATION	Feeling of extreme happiness or pleasure
ELUDED	Escaped from one's understanding
ENDURE	Carry on through hardships

EXHORTED	Urged through arguments or appeals
FLACCID	Lacking firmness or muscle tone
FOREBODING	Predicting something bad for the future
FUTILE	Useless
GRATIFY	Satisfy; indulge
HYSTERICAL	Having uncontrolled emotions

IMPALPABLE	Can't be grasped by touch or in the mind
IMPELLED	Motivated; had the feeling of needing to do something
IMPERIOUSLY	Overbearingly; pressingly; urgently
IMPLICATE	Connect incriminatingly
IMPULSE	Inclination; motivating force
IMPUTED	Attributed; credited

INARTICULATE	Wordless; speechless
INDELIBLE	Permanent
INEXTRICABLY	Not being able to escape from
IRKED	Irritated; bothered
IRREVOCABLE	Can't be taken or sent back
LABYRINTH	Maze

LATENT	Dormant; present but not active
LATITUDE	Leeway; freedom within regulations
LINGERING	Remaining, as though reluctant to leave
LULLED	Calmed
MITIGATING	Making more moderate
MORASS	Something that hinders, engulfs, or overwhelms

PEEVED	Vexed; angry
PREMEDITATION	Planning beforehand
QUEER	Strange
RENDERED	Made; caused to be
REPROACH	Disapproval
SANCTION	Approve

STAVE	Put off; postpone
SUBSIDED	Quieted; settled
SUCCUMB	Give in; come under the influence of
SULLEN	Sulky
SURLY	Bad-humored; gruff
TAUT	Tight; tense

UNABATING	Not subsiding; not becoming less
UNETHICAL	Wrong; not within accepted guidelines
VENUE	Location where a trial is held
VIGILANTES	People who take the law into their own hands
VOWED	Promised
YEARNING	Longing

Native Son Vocabulary

UNABATING	ARDENTLY	VOWED	EBBED	ACCORD
CONTAGION	ASPIRATION	IMPULSE	UNETHICAL	SUCCUMB
ELATION	FOREBODING	FREE SPACE	REPROACH	PEEVED
BELLIGERENTLY	IRREVOCABLE	ELUDED	EXHORTED	INARTICULATE
INEXTRICABLY	ENDURE	RENDERED	SANCTION	LATITUDE

Native Son Vocabulary

MORASS	LATENT	APPREHENSIVELY	AUGMENTED	STAVE
TAUT	QUEER	ALIBI	DUPED	ANARCHIST
ATONE	SUBSIDED	FREE SPACE	LABYRINTH	BENEVOLENT
IMPERIOUSLY	FLACCID	CONJECTURED	LINGERING	AWE
CONDEMNED	CONTRITE	IRKED	CONSENTED	MITIGATING

Native Son Vocabulary

ENDURE	MORASS	DUPED	YEARNING	IMPERIOUSLY
PEEVED	ARDENTLY	ARRAIGNMENT	SUBSIDED	INEXTRICABLY
BENEVOLENT	VOWED	FREE SPACE	PREMEDITATION	IMPLICATE
EBBED	QUEER	RENDERED	LINGERING	ELUDED
AWE	INARTICULATE	LABYRINTH	EXHORTED	ANARCHIST

Native Son Vocabulary

CONTRITE	IMPUTED	MITIGATING	SURLY	APPREHENSIVELY
CONTAGION	SULLEN	SUCCUMB	ALIBI	CONSENTED
ATONE	ASPIRATION	FREE SPACE	IRKED	SANCTION
BELLIGERENTLY	LATENT	IMPELLED	ABSTRACTEDLY	UNABATING
CONJECTURED	VIGILANTES	FLACCID	CONDEMNED	UNETHICAL

Native Son Vocabulary

DUPED	FOREBODING	ELATION	IRREVOCABLE	LINGERING
YEARNING	SURLY	IMPUTED	INDELIBLE	IMPERIOUSLY
LATITUDE	ASPIRATION	FREE SPACE	CONTRITE	BELLIGERENTLY
SANCTION	PEEVED	AWE	MORASS	ATONE
REPROACH	SULLEN	FUTILE	MITIGATING	IMPULSE

Native Son Vocabulary

LATENT	ANARCHIST	PREMEDITATION	ENDURE	SUBSIDED
HYSTERICAL	CONSENTED	ARRAIGNMENT	ELUDED	LABYRINTH
LULLED	IRKED	FREE SPACE	GRATIFY	RENDERED
EXHORTED	BENEVOLENT	DORMANT	VOWED	TAUT
CONDEMNED	EBBED	AUGMENTED	CONJECTURED	APPREHENSIVELY

Native Son Vocabulary

ASPIRATION	QUEER	FOREBODING	IMPLICATE	CONJECTURED
ACCORD	IMPERIOUSLY	VOWED	BENEVOLENT	ELATION
ENDURE	VENUE	FREE SPACE	SULLEN	GRATIFY
LATITUDE	IRREVOCABLE	UNABATING	CONTRITE	BELLIGERENTLY
CONTAGION	CONDEMNED	MITIGATING	REPROACH	LINGERING

Native Son Vocabulary

AUGMENTED	SURLY	VIGILANTES	INARTICULATE	ANARCHIST
SUCCUMB	HYSTERICAL	ABSTRACTEDLY	FUTILE	EBBED
STAVE	SUBSIDED	FREE SPACE	INDELIBLE	IRKED
SANCTION	EXHORTED	IMPUTED	TAUT	ARRAIGNMENT
PREMEDITATION	IMPALPABLE	INEXTRICABLY	RENDERED	FLACCID

Native Son Vocabulary

APPREHENSIVELY	VENUE	CONJECTURED	STAVE	REPROACH
DORMANT	FOREBODING	VOWED	INEXTRICABLY	ARDENTLY
SUCCUMB	ELATION	FREE SPACE	LATITUDE	ELUDED
PEEVED	TAUT	INARTICULATE	EBBED	ABSTRACTEDLY
INDELIBLE	IRKED	ATONE	LINGERING	IMPALPABLE

Native Son Vocabulary

LABYRINTH	IMPLICATE	CONTAGION	ACCORD	IMPULSE
UNABATING	PREMEDITATION	FUTILE	CONSENTED	BENEVOLENT
ALIBI	ARRAIGNMENT	FREE SPACE	IMPELLED	BELLIGERENTLY
FLACCID	AUGMENTED	CONDEMNED	RENDERED	MITIGATING
ANARCHIST	CONTRITE	GRATIFY	DUPED	VIGILANTES

Native Son Vocabulary

FUTILE	INEXTRICABLY	LULLED	EBBED	LINGERING
ARRAIGNMENT	EXHORTED	AWE	SURLY	MITIGATING
TAUT	YEARNING	FREE SPACE	CONSENTED	IMPUTED
CONJECTURED	IMPALPABLE	FLACCID	SANCTION	IMPULSE
PEEVED	DUPED	CONDEMNED	INDELIBLE	ACCORD

Native Son Vocabulary

HYSTERICAL	SUCCUMB	IMPLICATE	CONTAGION	DORMANT
BELLIGERENTLY	UNABATING	REPROACH	PREMEDITATION	GRATIFY
MORASS	ALIBI	FREE SPACE	CONTRITE	APPREHENSIVELY
IMPERIOUSLY	LABYRINTH	VOWED	ARDENTLY	LATENT
SULLEN	AUGMENTED	QUEER	ATONE	IRKED

Native Son Vocabulary

SUCCUMB	FLACCID	INEXTRICABLY	GRATIFY	ACCORD
MITIGATING	DORMANT	MORASS	ATONE	LULLED
SANCTION	ANARCHIST	FREE SPACE	PEEVED	ENDURE
CONDEMNED	LABYRINTH	SULLEN	QUEER	CONTAGION
FOREBODING	APPREHENSIVELY	TAUT	LATENT	YEARNING

Native Son Vocabulary

CONJECTURED	BENEVOLENT	PREMEDITATION	SURLY	AWE
FUTILE	CONTRITE	IRREVOCABLE	INARTICULATE	IMPALPABLE
VENUE	VIGILANTES	FREE SPACE	IMPERIOUSLY	IMPULSE
ALIBI	ARDENTLY	UNETHICAL	LATITUDE	HYSTERICAL
CONSENTED	IMPLICATE	BELLIGERENTLY	LINGERING	ABSTRACTEDLY

Native Son Vocabulary

QUEER	RENDERED	ABSTRACTEDLY	SANCTION	GRATIFY
SUCCUMB	BENEVOLENT	PEEVED	AUGMENTED	INDELIBLE
LULLED	IMPULSE	FREE SPACE	LABYRINTH	ENDURE
SUBSIDED	CONTAGION	IMPUTED	UNABATING	UNETHICAL
IRREVOCABLE	SURLY	REPROACH	INEXTRICABLY	ARDENTLY

Native Son Vocabulary

IMPELLED	FLACCID	LATENT	STAVE	BELLIGERENTLY
EBBED	ACCORD	FOREBODING	CONTRITE	IMPLICATE
MORASS	HYSTERICAL	FREE SPACE	ELATION	MITIGATING
YEARNING	ANARCHIST	LINGERING	EXHORTED	AWE
VIGILANTES	TAUT	CONDEMNED	ARRAIGNMENT	DORMANT

Native Son Vocabulary

ARRAIGNMENT	ACCORD	PEEVED	EBBED	APPREHENSIVELY
LATITUDE	GRATIFY	FLACCID	FOREBODING	DUPED
CONTRITE	ANARCHIST	FREE SPACE	ELUDED	ELATION
IRREVOCABLE	FUTILE	ENDURE	VENUE	VIGILANTES
INDELIBLE	SUBSIDED	TAUT	LINGERING	LATENT

Native Son Vocabulary

YEARNING	ALIBI	ATONE	AUGMENTED	ABSTRACTEDLY
IMPELLED	STAVE	IMPUTED	IMPALPABLE	LABYRINTH
AWE	RENDERED	FREE SPACE	QUEER	DORMANT
ASPIRATION	CONJECTURED	LULLED	REPROACH	IMPULSE
SANCTION	UNABATING	SUCCUMB	CONDEMNED	IRKED

Native Son Vocabulary

LABYRINTH	VIGILANTES	BELLIGERENTLY	FOREBODING	ASPIRATION
IMPLICATE	PEEVED	REPROACH	ATONE	STAVE
IMPUTED	ENDURE	FREE SPACE	UNETHICAL	VENUE
ALIBI	AWE	IMPELLED	MORASS	INEXTRICABLY
IMPERIOUSLY	VOWED	ANARCHIST	LATITUDE	ABSTRACTEDLY

Native Son Vocabulary

DUPED	INDELIBLE	EBBED	SUBSIDED	ELATION
ELUDED	CONJECTURED	CONSENTED	ARRAIGNMENT	HYSTERICAL
TAUT	IRREVOCABLE	FREE SPACE	PREMEDITATION	QUEER
CONDEMNED	LATENT	SURLY	ACCORD	YEARNING
SULLEN	INARTICULATE	LINGERING	FLACCID	FUTILE

Native Son Vocabulary

ENDURE	LATITUDE	CONTRITE	LINGERING	FUTILE
PREMEDITATION	DORMANT	DUPED	VENUE	INEXTRICABLY
AWE	IMPALPABLE	FREE SPACE	IMPERIOUSLY	EXHORTED
BENEVOLENT	GRATIFY	ANARCHIST	CONTAGION	RENDERED
ASPIRATION	SANCTION	ALIBI	ELATION	REPROACH

Native Son Vocabulary

ACCORD	ELUDED	LATENT	VOWED	SUCCUMB
STAVE	IRREVOCABLE	FOREBODING	IRKED	QUEER
MORASS	IMPUTED	FREE SPACE	EBBED	LULLED
UNABATING	ARDENTLY	SURLY	IMPELLED	IMPLICATE
HYSTERICAL	APPREHENSIVELY	ARRAIGNMENT	SUBSIDED	CONSENTED

Native Son Vocabulary

IRKED	CONDEMNED	TAUT	ASPIRATION	INARTICULATE
ARRAIGNMENT	MORASS	BENEVOLENT	DORMANT	CONJECTURED
ABSTRACTEDLY	IMPELLED	FREE SPACE	HYSTERICAL	PEEVED
SULLEN	AWE	EXHORTED	IMPULSE	QUEER
MITIGATING	GRATIFY	FUTILE	CONTRITE	CONTAGION

Native Son Vocabulary

PREMEDITATION	LULLED	RENDERED	STAVE	ELUDED
ATONE	LABYRINTH	IMPALPABLE	UNABATING	VENUE
VOWED	FLACCID	FREE SPACE	APPREHENSIVELY	ANARCHIST
SURLY	IRREVOCABLE	INDELIBLE	LATITUDE	LATENT
INEXTRICABLY	IMPERIOUSLY	FOREBODING	SUCCUMB	AUGMENTED

Native Son Vocabulary

IMPLICATE	ALIBI	CONTRITE	CONJECTURED	INARTICULATE
IMPULSE	UNETHICAL	SUCCUMB	RENDERED	ELUDED
FLACCID	SUBSIDED	FREE SPACE	LINGERING	ANARCHIST
LATENT	EBBED	LABYRINTH	LULLED	APPREHENSIVELY
FOREBODING	DUPED	CONTAGION	CONDEMNED	ENDURE

Native Son Vocabulary

ELATION	INEXTRICABLY	ARRAIGNMENT	BELLIGERENTLY	SANCTION
BENEVOLENT	MITIGATING	YEARNING	AWE	LATITUDE
IMPELLED	IMPALPABLE	FREE SPACE	VOWED	PREMEDITATION
ABSTRACTEDLY	ACCORD	SURLY	IRREVOCABLE	PEEVED
IMPUTED	INDELIBLE	AUGMENTED	VIGILANTES	EXHORTED

Native Son Vocabulary

QUEER	UNABATING	IMPULSE	GRATIFY	TAUT
IMPUTED	SULLEN	PEEVED	ABSTRACTEDLY	LINGERING
CONTRITE	VOWED	FREE SPACE	ELUDED	ASPIRATION
SANCTION	ATONE	REPROACH	ARRAIGNMENT	CONSENTED
INDELIBLE	STAVE	EBBED	ELATION	UNETHICAL

Native Son Vocabulary

IRREVOCABLE	VIGILANTES	LATITUDE	INEXTRICABLY	MORASS
SUBSIDED	YEARNING	FOREBODING	MITIGATING	DORMANT
IMPALPABLE	IRKED	FREE SPACE	PREMEDITATION	EXHORTED
SURLY	IMPERIOUSLY	INARTICULATE	CONJECTURED	CONDEMNED
BENEVOLENT	LULLED	CONTAGION	IMPELLED	ARDENTLY

Native Son Vocabulary

ABSTRACTEDLY	CONTRITE	FOREBODING	TAUT	ARDENTLY
EXHORTED	DUPED	IMPERIOUSLY	PREMEDITATION	INARTICULATE
IMPALPABLE	INEXTRICABLY	FREE SPACE	VIGILANTES	LULLED
ARRAIGNMENT	BELLIGERENTLY	CONDEMNED	IMPELLED	REPROACH
ENDURE	UNETHICAL	CONSENTED	FUTILE	HYSTERICAL

Native Son Vocabulary

BENEVOLENT	CONJECTURED	LATENT	ANARCHIST	IRREVOCABLE
ASPIRATION	MORASS	ELATION	EBBED	IRKED
IMPLICATE	VENUE	FREE SPACE	FLACCID	AWE
MITIGATING	YEARNING	SUBSIDED	AUGMENTED	STAVE
SUCCUMB	VOWED	RENDERED	SURLY	LATITUDE

Native Son Vocabulary

IMPLICATE	HYSTERICAL	UNABATING	ASPIRATION	INEXTRICABLY
PEEVED	LULLED	CONDEMNED	YEARNING	BENEVOLENT
ATONE	ALIBI	FREE SPACE	TAUT	VOWED
SUBSIDED	LATENT	IRKED	IMPUTED	DORMANT
SUCCUMB	STAVE	CONJECTURED	CONTRITE	IMPALPABLE

Native Son Vocabulary

FUTILE	UNETHICAL	REPROACH	ELUDED	CONSENTED
MORASS	SULLEN	GRATIFY	EBBED	LABYRINTH
MITIGATING	LATITUDE	FREE SPACE	INDELIBLE	LINGERING
AWE	BELLIGERENTLY	CONTAGION	FLACCID	SANCTION
FOREBODING	IRREVOCABLE	EXHORTED	ARDENTLY	IMPULSE

www.ingramcontent.com/pod-product-compliance
Lightning Source LLC
Chambersburg PA
CBHW081454070526
44586CB00019B/2352